PENGUIN

METAMORPHOSI...

S0-AWN-061

Franz Kafka was born in Prague in 1883, the son of a rich Jewish Czech merchant. After studying literature and medicine for a short time, he turned to law, which he believed was the profession that would give him the greatest amount of free time for his private life and for his writing. He took his doctorate in law at Prague University, got a job with an insurance company, and later became a clerk in the semi-governmental Workers' Insurance Office. In later years the necessity of earning his living by routine office work became an intolerable burden, and he broke away altogether, settling down in a Berlin suburb to devote himself to writing. In 1914 he became engaged, but broke it off, feeling unable to face marriage. He made one more attempt to marry, but it was discovered that he was suffering from tuberculosis and he went to a sanatorium. His unsatisfactory love affairs, his relationship with his father, a self-made man who cared nothing for his son's literary aspirations, and his own inflexible intellectual honesty and almost psychopathic sensitivity finally broke down his health and the 'hunger years' of post-1918 Berlin added the finishing touches. He died in 1924. Although a Czech, Kafka's books were all written in German. Seven of them were published during his lifetime. *The Trial* first appeared after the author's death in 1925, *The Castle* in 1926, *America* in 1927, and *The Great Wall of China* in 1931.

FRANZ KAFKA

Metamorphosis

AND OTHER STORIES

TRANSLATED BY
WILLA AND EDWIN
MUIR

PENGUIN BOOKS

Penguin Books Ltd, Harmondsworth, Middlesex, England
Penguin Books Australia Ltd, Ringwood, Victoria, Australia

—

Die Verwandlung (Metamorphosis) first published 1916
Beim Bau der Chinesischen Mauer (The Great Wall of China)
first published 1931
Forschungen eines Hundes (Investigations of a Dog) first published 1931
Des Bau (The Burrow) first published 1931
In der Strafkolonie (In the Penal Settlement) first published 1919
Der Riesenmaulwurf (The Giant Mole) first published 1931

—

Metamorphosis (under the title *The Transformation*) and *In the
Penal Settlement* first published in this translation 1933

—

This selection first published in Penguin Books 1961
Reprinted 1963, 1964, 1965, 1967, 1968, 1970, 1971 (twice), 1972

—

Made and printed in Great Britain
by Hazell Watson & Viney Ltd,
Aylesbury, Bucks
Set in Monotype Romulus

CONTENTS

Metamorphosis

As Gregor Samsa awoke one morning from uneasy dreams he found himself transformed in his bed into a gigantic insect. He was lying on his hard, as it were armour-plated, back and when he lifted his head a little he could see his dome-like brown belly divided into stiff arched segments on top of which the bed-quilt could hardly keep in position and was about to slide off completely. His numerous legs, which were pitifully thin compared to the rest of his bulk, waved helplessly before his eyes.

What has happened to me? he thought. It was no dream. His room, a regular human bedroom, only rather too small, lay quiet between the four familiar walls. Above the table on which a collection of cloth samples was unpacked and spread out – Samsa was a commercial traveller – hung the picture which he had recently cut out of an illustrated magazine and put into a pretty gilt frame. It showed a lady, with a fur cap on and a fur stole, sitting upright and holding out to the spectator a huge fur muff into which the whole of her forearm had vanished.

Gregor's eyes turned next to the window, and the overcast sky – one could hear raindrops beating on the window gutter – made him quite melancholy. What about sleeping a little longer and forgetting all this nonsense, he thought, but it could not be done, for he was accustomed to sleep on his right side and in his present condition he could not turn himself over. However violently he forced himself towards his right side he always rolled on to his back again. He tried it at least a hundred times, shutting his eyes to keep from seeing his struggling legs, and only desisted when he began to feel in his side a faint dull ache he had never experienced before.

O God, he thought, what an exhausting job I've picked on! Travelling about day in, day out. It's much more irritating work than doing the actual business in the warehouse, and on top of that there's the trouble of constant travelling, of worrying about train connexions, the bed and irregular meals, casual acquaintances that are always new and never become intimate friends. The devil take it all! He felt a slight itching up on his belly; slowly pushed himself on his back nearer to the top of the bed so that he could lift his head more easily; identified the itching place which was surrounded by many small white spots the nature of which he could not understand, and made to touch it with a leg, but drew the leg back immediately, for the contact made a cold shiver run through him.

He slid down again into his former position. This getting up early, he thought, makes one quite stupid. A man needs his sleep. Other commercials live like harem women. For instance, when I come back to the hotel of a morning to write up the orders I've got, these others are only sitting down to breakfast. Let me just try that on with my chief; I'd be sacked on the spot. Anyhow, that might be quite a good thing for me, who can tell? If I didn't have to hold my hand because of my parents I'd have given notice long ago, I'd have gone to the chief and told him exactly what I think of him. That would knock him endways from his desk! It's a queer way of acting, too, this sitting on high at a desk and talking down to employees, especially when they have to come quite near because the chief is hard of hearing. Well, there's still hope; once I've saved enough money to pay back my parents' debts to him – that should take another five or six years – I'll do it without fail. I'll cut myself completely loose then. For the moment, though, I'd better get up, since my train goes at five.

He looked at the alarm-clock ticking on the chest. Heavenly Father! he thought. It was half past six o'clock and the hands were quietly moving on, it was even past the half hour, it was getting on for a quarter to seven. Had the alarm-clock not gone off? From the bed one could see that it had been properly set for four o'clock; of course it must have gone off. Yes, but was it possible to sleep quietly through that ear-splitting noise? Well, he had not slept quietly, yet apparently all the more soundly for that. But what was he to do now? The next train went at seven o'clock; to catch that he would need to hurry like mad and his samples weren't even packed up, and he himself wasn't feeling particularly fresh and active. And even if he did catch the train he wouldn't avoid a row with the chief, since the warehouse porter would have been waiting for the five o'clock train and would have long since reported his failure to turn up. The porter was a creature of the chief's, spineless and stupid. Well, supposing he were to say he was sick? But that would be most unpleasant and would look suspicious, since during his five years' employment he had not been ill once. The chief himself would be sure to come with the sick-insurance doctor, would reproach his parents with their son's laziness, and would cut all excuses short by referring to the insurance doctor, who of course regarded all mankind as perfectly healthy malingerers. And would he be so far wrong on this occasion? Gregor really felt quite well, apart from a drowsiness that was utterly superfluous after such a long sleep, and he was even unusually hungry.

As all this was running through his mind at top speed without his being able to decide to leave his bed – the alarm-clock had just struck a quarter to seven – there came a cautious tap at the door behind the head of his bed. 'Gregor,' said a voice – it was his mother's – 'it's a quarter to seven. Hadn't you a train to catch?' That gentle voice! Gregor had a shock as he heard his own voice answering hers, unmistakably his own voice, it was true, but with a persistent horrible twittering squeak behind it like an undertone, that left the words in their clear shape only for the first moment and then rose up reverberating round them to destroy their sense, so that one could not be sure one had heard them rightly. Gregor wanted to answer at length and explain everything, but in the circumstances he confined himself to saying: 'Yes, yes, thank you, mother, I'm getting up now.' The wooden door between them must have kept the change in his voice from being noticeable outside, for his mother contented herself with this statement and shuffled away. Yet this brief exchange of words had made the other members of the family aware that Gregor was still in the house, as they had not expected, and at one of the side-doors his father was already knocking, gently, yet with his fist. 'Gregor, Gregor,' he called, 'what's the matter with you?' And after a little while he called again in a deeper voice: 'Gregor! Gregor!' At the other side-door his sister was saying in a low, plaintive tone: 'Gregor? Aren't you well? Are you needing anything?' He answered them both at once: 'I'm just ready,' and did his best to make his voice sound as normal as possible by enunciating the words very clearly and leaving long pauses between them. So his father went back to his breakfast, but his sister whispered: 'Gregor, open the door, do.' However, he was not thinking of opening the door, and felt thankful for the prudent habit he had acquired in travelling of locking all doors during the night, even at home.

His immediate intention was to get up quietly without being disturbed, to put on his clothes and above all eat his breakfast, and only then to consider what else was to be done, since in bed, he was well aware, his meditations would come to no sensible conclusion. He remembered that often enough in bed he had felt small aches and pains, probably caused by awkward postures, which had proved purely imaginary once he got up, and he looked forward eagerly to seeing this morning's delusions gradually fall away. That the change in his voice was nothing but the precursor of a severe chill, a standing ailment of commercial travellers, he had not the least possible doubt.

To get rid of the quilt was quite easy; he had only to inflate himself a little and it fell off by itself. But the next move was difficult, especially because he was so uncommonly broad. He would have needed arms and hands to hoist himself up; instead he had only the numerous little legs which never stopped waving in all directions and which he could not control in the least.

When he tried to bend one of them it was the first to stretch it-self straight; and did he succeed at last in making it do what he wanted, all the other legs meanwhile waved the more wildly in a high degree of unpleasant agitation. 'But what's the use of lying idle in bed,' said Gregor to himself.

He thought that he might get out of bed with the lower part of his body first, but this lower part, which he had not yet seen and of which he could form no clear conception, proved too difficult to move; it shifted so slowly; and when finally, almost wild with annoyance, he gathered his forces together and thrust out recklessly, he had miscalculated the direction and bumped heavily against the lower end of the bed, and the stinging pain he felt informed him that precisely this lower part of his body was at the moment probably the most sensitive.

So he tried to get the top part of himself out first, and cautiously moved his head towards the edge of the bed. That proved easy enough, and despite its breadth and mass the bulk of his body at last slowly followed the movement of his head. Still, when he finally got his head free over the edge of the bed he felt too scared to go on advancing, for after all if he let him-self fall in this way it would take a miracle to keep his head from being injured. And at all costs he must not lose conscious-ness now, precisely now; he would rather stay in bed.

But when after a repetition of the same efforts he lay in his former position again, sighing, and watched his little legs struggling against each other more wildly than ever, if that were possible, and saw no way of bringing any order into this arbitrary confusion, he told himself again that it was impossible to stay in bed and that the most sensible course was to risk everything for the smallest hope of getting away from it. At the same time he did not forget meanwhile to remind himself that cool reflection, the coolest possible, was much better than desperate resolves. In such moments he focused his eyes as sharply as possible on the window, but, unfortunately, the prospect of the morning fog, which muffled even the other side of the narrow street, brought him little encouragement and comfort. 'Seven o'clock already,' he said to himself when the alarm-clock chimed again, 'seven o'clock already and still such a thick fog.' And for a little while he lay quiet, breathing lightly, as if perhaps expecting such complete repose to restore all things to their real and normal condition.

But then he said to himself: 'Before it strikes a quarter past seven I must be quite out of this bed, without fail. Anyhow, by that time someone will have come from the warehouse to ask for me, since it opens before seven.' And he set himself to rocking his whole body at once in a regular rhythm, with the idea of swinging it out of the bed. If he tipped himself out in that way he could keep his head from injury by lifting it at an acute angle when he fell. His back seemed to be hard and was not likely to suffer from a fall on the carpet. His biggest worry was the loud crash he would not be able to help making, which would probably cause anxiety, if not terror, behind all the doors. Still, he must take the risk.

When he was already half out of the bed – the new method was more a game than an effort, for he needed only to hitch himself across by rocking to and fro – it struck him how simple it would be if he could get help. Two strong people – he thought of his father and the servant girl – would be amply sufficient; they would only have to thrust their arms under his convex back, lever him out of the bed, bend down with their burden and then be patient enough to let him turn himself right over on to the floor, where it was to be hoped his legs would then find their proper function. Well, ignoring the fact that the doors were all locked, ought he really to call for help? In spite of his misery he could not suppress a smile at the very idea of it.

He had got so far that he could barely keep his equilibrium when he rocked himself strongly, and he would have to nerve himself very soon for the final decision since in five minutes' time it would be a quarter past seven – when the front-door bell rang. 'That's someone from the warehouse,' he said to himself and grew almost rigid, while his little legs only jigged about all the faster. For a moment everything stayed quiet. 'They're not going to open the door,' said Gregor to himself, catching at some kind of irrational hope. But then of course the servant girl went as usual to the door with her heavy tread and opened it. Gregor needed only to hear the first 'good morning' of the visitor to know immediately who it was – the chief clerk himself. What a fate, to be condemned to work for a firm where the smallest omission at once gave rise to the gravest suspicion! Were all employees in a body nothing but scoundrels, was there not among them one single loyal devoted man, who, though he might have wasted an hour or so of the firm's time in a morning, was so tormented by conscience as to be driven out of his mind and actually incapable of leaving his bed? Wouldn't it really have been sufficient to send an apprentice to inquire – if any inquiry were necessary at all – did the chief clerk himself have to come and thus indicate to the entire family, an innocent family, that this suspicious circumstance could be investigated by no one less versed in affairs than himself? And more through the agitation caused by these reflections than through any act of will Gregor swung himself out of bed with all his strength. There was a loud thump, but it was not really a crash. His fall was broken to some extent by the carpet, his back, too, was less stiff than he thought, and so there was merely a dull thud, not so very startling. Only he had not lifted his head carefully enough and had hit it; he turned it and rubbed it on the carpet in pain and irritation.

'That was something falling down in there,' said the chief clerk in the next room to the left. Gregor tried to suppose to himself that something like what had happened to him today might some day happen to the chief clerk; one really could not deny that it was possible. But as if in brusque reply to this supposition the chief clerk took a couple of firm steps in the next-door room and his patent leather boots creaked. From the right-hand room his sister was whispering to inform him of

the situation: 'Gregor, the chief clerk's here.' 'I know,' mut-
tered Gregor to himself; but he didn't dare to make his voice
loud enough for his sister to hear it.

'Gregor,' said his father now from the left-hand room, 'the
chief clerk has come and wants to know why you didn't catch
the early train. We don't know what to say to him. Besides, he
wants to talk to you in person. So open the door, please. He
will be good enough to excuse the untidiness of your room.'

'Good morning, Mr Samsa,' the chief clerk was calling amiably meanwhile. 'He's not well,' said his mother to the visitor,
while his father was still speaking through the door. 'He's not
well, sir, believe me. What else would make him miss a train!
The boy thinks about nothing but his work. It makes me
almost cross, the way he never goes out in the evenings, he's
been here the last eight days and has stayed at home every
single evening. He just sits there quietly at the table reading a
newspaper or looking through railway time-tables. The only
amusement he gets is doing fret-work. For instance, he spent
two or three evenings cutting out a little picture-frame; you
would be surprised to see how pretty it is; it's hanging in his
room, you'll see it in a minute when Gregor opens the door. I
must say I'm glad you've come, sir; we should never have got
him to unlock the door by ourselves; he's so obstinate; and
I'm sure he's unwell, though he wouldn't have it to be so this
morning.' 'I'm just coming,' said Gregor slowly and carefully,
not moving an inch for fear of losing one word of the conversation. 'I can't think of any other explanation, madam,' said the
chief clerk: 'I hope it's nothing serious. Although on the other
hand I must say that we men of business – fortunately or unfortunately – very often simply have to ignore any slight indisposition, since business must be attended to.' 'Well, can the
chief clerk come in now?' asked Gregor's father impatiently,
again knocking on the door. 'No,' said Gregor. In the left-hand
room a painful silence followed this refusal, in the right-hand
room his sister began to sob.

Why didn't his sister join the others? She was probably newly out of bed and hadn't even begun to put on her clothes yet. Well, why was she crying? Because he wouldn't get up and let the chief clerk in, because he was in danger of losing his job, and because the chief would begin dunning his parents again for the old debts? Surely these were things one didn't need to worry about for the present. Gregor was still at home and not in the least thinking of deserting the family. At the moment, true, he was lying on the carpet and no one who knew the condition he was in could seriously expect him to admit the chief clerk. But for such a small discourtesy, which could plausibly be explained away somehow later on, Gregor could hardly be dismissed on the spot. And it seemed to Gregor that it would be much more sensible to leave him in peace for the present than to trouble him with tears and entreaties. Still, of course, their uncertainty bewildered them all and excused their behaviour.

'Mr Samsa,' the chief clerk called now in a louder voice, 'what's the matter with you? Here you are, barricading yourself in your room, giving only "yes" and "no" for answers, causing your parents a lot of unnecessary trouble and neglecting – I mention this only in passing – neglecting your business duties in an incredible fashion. I am speaking here in the name of your parents and of your chief, and I beg you quite seriously to give me an immediate and precise explanation. You amaze me, you amaze me. I thought you were a quiet, dependable person, and now all at once you seem bent on making a disgraceful exhibition of yourself. The chief did hint to me early this morning a possible explanation for your disappearance – with reference to the cash payments that were entrusted to you recently – but I almost pledged my solemn word of honour that this could not be so. But now that I see how incredibly obstinate you are, I no longer have the slightest desire to take your part at all. And your position in the firm is not so unassailable. I came with the intention of telling you all this in private, but since you are wasting my time so needlessly I don't see why your parents shouldn't hear it too. For some time past your work has been most unsatisfactory; this is not the season of the year for a business boom, of course, we admit that, but a season of the year for doing no business at all, that does not exist, Mr Samsa, must not exist.'

'But, sir,' cried Gregor, beside himself and in his agitation forgetting everything else, 'I'm just going to open the door this very minute. A slight illness, an attack of giddiness, has kept me from getting up. I'm still lying in bed. But I feel all right again. I'm getting out of bed now. Just give me a moment or two longer! I'm not quite so well as I thought. But I'm all right, really. How a thing like that can suddenly strike one down! Only last night I was quite well, my parents can tell you, or rather I did have a slight presentiment. I must have showed some sign of it. Why didn't I report it at the warehouse! But one always thinks that an indisposition can be got over without staying in the house. Oh sir, do spare my parents! All that you're reproaching me with now has no foundation; no one has ever said a word to me about it. Perhaps you haven't looked at the last orders I sent in. Anyhow, I can still catch the eight o'clock train, I'm much the better for my few hours' rest. Don't let me detain you here, sir; I'll be attending to business very soon, and do be good enough to tell the chief so and to make my excuses to him!'

And while all this was tumbling out pell-mell and Gregor hardly knew what he was saying, he had reached the chest quite easily, perhaps because of the practice he had had in bed, and was now trying to lever himself upright by means of it. He meant actually to open the door, actually to show himself and speak to the chief clerk; he was eager to find out what the others, after all their insistence, would say at the sight of him. If they were horrified then the responsibility was no longer his and he could stay quiet. But if they took it calmly, then he had no reason either to be upset, and could really get to the station for the eight o'clock train if he hurried. At first he slipped down a few times from the polished surface of the chest, but at length with a last heave he stood upright; he paid no more attention to the pains in the lower part of his body, however they smarted. Then he let himself fall against the back of a near-by chair, and clung with his little legs to the edges of it. That brought him into control of himself again and he stopped speaking, for now he could listen to what the chief clerk was saying.

'Did you understand a word of it?' the chief clerk was asking; 'surely he can't be trying to make fools of us?' 'Oh dear,' cried his mother, in tears, 'perhaps he's terribly ill and we're tormenting him. Grete! Grete!' she called out then. 'Yes, mother?' called his sister from the other side. They were calling to each other across Gregor's room. 'You must go this minute for the doctor. Gregor is ill. Go for the doctor, quick. Did you hear how he was speaking?' 'That was no human voice,' said the chief clerk in a voice noticeably low beside the shrillness of the mother's. 'Anna! Anna!' his father was calling through the hall to the kitchen, clapping his hands, 'get a locksmith at once!' And the two girls were already running through the hall with a swish of skirts – how could his sister have got dressed so quickly? – and were tearing the front door open. There was no sound of its closing again; they had evidently left it open, as one does in houses where some great misfortune has happened.

But Gregor was now much calmer. The words he uttered were no longer understandable, apparently, although they seemed clear enough to him, even clearer than before, perhaps because his ear had grown accustomed to the sound of them. Yet at any rate people now believed that something was wrong with him, and were ready to help him. The positive certainty with which these first measures had been taken comforted him. He felt himself drawn once more into the human circle and hoped for great and remarkable results from both the doctor and the locksmith, without really distinguishing precisely between them. To make his voice as clear as possible for the decisive conversation that was now imminent he coughed a little, as quietly as he could, of course, since this noise too might not sound like a human cough for all he was able to judge. In the next room meanwhile there was complete silence. Perhaps his parents were sitting at the table with the chief clerk, whispering, perhaps they were all leaning against the door and listening.

Slowly Gregor pushed the chair towards the door, then let go of it, caught hold of the door for support – the soles at the end of his little legs were somewhat sticky – and rested against it for a moment after his efforts. Then he set himself to turning the key in the lock with his mouth. It seemed, unhappily, that he hadn't really any teeth – what could he grip the key with? – but on the other hand his jaws were certainly very strong; with their help he did manage to set the key in motion, heedless of the fact that he was undoubtedly damaging them somewhere, since a brown fluid issued from his mouth, flowed over the key and dripped on the floor. 'Just listen to that,' said the chief clerk next door; 'he's turning the key.' That was a great encouragement to Gregor; but they should all have shouted encouragement to him, his father and mother too: 'Go on, Gregor,' they should have called out, 'keep going, hold on to that key!' And in the belief that they were all following his efforts intently, he clenched his jaws recklessly on the key with all the force at his command. As the turning of the key progressed he circled round the lock, holding on now only with his mouth, pushing on the key, as required, or pulling it down again with all the weight of his body. The louder click of the finally yielding lock literally quickened Gregor. With a deep breath of relief he said to himself: 'So I didn't need the locksmith,' and laid his head on the handle to open the door wide.

Since he had to pull the door towards him, he was still invisible when it was really wide open. He had to edge himself slowly round the near half of the double door, and to do it very carefully if he was not to fall plump upon his back just on the threshold. He was still carrying out this difficult manoeuvre with no time to observe anything else, when he heard the chief clerk utter a loud 'Oh!' – it sounded like a gust of wind – and now he could see the man, standing as he was nearest to the door, clapping one hand before his open mouth and slowly backing away as if driven by some invisible steady pressure. His mother – in spite of the chief clerk's being there her hair was still undone and sticking up in all directions – first clasped her hands and looked at his father, then took two steps towards Gregor and fell on the floor among her outspread skirts, her face quite hidden on her breast. His father knotted his fist with a fierce expression on his face as if he meant to knock Gregor back into his room, then looked uncertainly round the living-room, covered his eyes with his hands and wept till his great chest heaved.

Gregor did not go now into the living-room, but leaned against the inside of the firmly shut wing of the door, so that only half his body was visible and his head above it bending sideways to look at the others. The light had meanwhile strengthened; on the other side of the street one could see clearly a section of the endlessly long, dark grey building op-posite – it was a hospital – abruptly punctuated by its row of regular windows; the rain was still falling, but only in large singly discernible and literally singly splashing drops. The breakfast dishes were set out on the table lavishly, for breakfast was the most important meal of the day to Gregor's father, who lingered it out for hours over various newspapers. Right op-posite Gregor on the wall hung a photograph of himself on military service, as a lieutenant, hand on sword, a carefree smile on his face, inviting one to respect his uniform and military bearing. The door leading to the hall was open, and one could see that the front door stood open too, showing the landing beyond and the beginning of the stairs going down.

'Well,' said Gregor, knowing perfectly that he was the only one who had retained any composure, 'I'll put my clothes on at once, pack up my samples and start off. Will you only let me go?

You see, sir, I'm not obstinate, and I'm willing to work; travelling is a hard life, but I couldn't live without it. Where are you going, sir? To the office? Yes? Will you give a true account of all this? One can be temporarily incapacitated, but that's just the moment for remembering former services and bearing in mind that later on, when the incapacity has been got over, one will certainly work with all the more industry and concentration. I'm loyally bound to serve the chief, you know that very well. Besides, I have to provide for my parents and my sister. I'm in great difficulties, but I'll get out of them again. Don't make things any worse for me than they are. Stand up for me in the firm. Travellers are not popular there, I know. People think they earn sacks of money and just have a good time. A prejudice there's no particular reason for revising. But you, sir, have a more comprehensive view of affairs than the rest of the staff, yes, let me tell you in confidence, a more comprehensive view than the chief himself, who, being the owner, lets his judgement easily be swayed against one of his employees. And you know very well that the traveller who is never seen in the office almost the whole year round, can so easily fall victim to gossip and ill luck and unfounded complaints, which he mostly knows nothing about, except when he comes back exhausted from his rounds, and only then suffers in person from their evil consequences, which he can no longer trace back to the original causes. Sir, sir, don't go away without a word to me to show that you think me in the right, at least to some extent!'

But at Gregor's very first words the chief clerk had already backed away and only stared at him with parted lips over one twitching shoulder. And while Gregor was speaking he did not stand still one moment but stole away towards the door, without taking his eyes off Gregor, yet only an inch at a time, as if obeying some secret injunction to leave the room. He was already at the hall, and the suddenness with which he took his last step out of the living-room would have made one believe he had burned the sole of his foot. Once in the hall he stretched his right arm before him towards the staircase, as if some supernatural power were waiting there to deliver him.

Gregor perceived that the chief clerk must on no account be allowed to go away in this frame of mind if his position in the firm were not to be endangered to the utmost. His parents did not understand this so well; they had convinced themselves in the course of years that Gregor was settled for life in this firm, and besides they were so preoccupied with their immediate troubles that all foresight had forsaken them. Yet Gregor had this foresight. The chief clerk must be detained, soothed, persuaded and finally won over; the whole future of Gregor and his family depended on it! If only his sister had been there! She was intelligent; she had begun to cry while Gregor was still lying quietly on his back. And no doubt the chief clerk, so partial to ladies, would have been guided by her; she would have shut the door of the flat and in the hall talked him out of his horror. But she was not there, and Gregor would have to handle the situation himself. And without remembering that he was still unaware what powers of movement he possessed, without even remembering that his words in all possibility, indeed in all likelihood, would again be unintelligible, he let go the wing of the door; pushed himself through the opening; started to walk towards the chief clerk, who was already ridiculously clinging with both hands to the railing on the landing: but immediately, as he was feeling for a support, he fell down with a little cry upon all his numerous legs. Hardly was he down when he experienced for the first time this morning a sense of physical comfort; his legs had firm ground under them; they were completely obedient, as he noted with joy; they even strove to carry him forward in whatever direction he chose; and he was inclined to believe that a final relief from all his sufferings was at hand. But in the same moment as he found himself on the floor, rocking with suppressed eagerness to move, not far from his mother, indeed just in front of her, she, who had seemed so completely crushed, sprang all at once to her feet, her

arms and fingers outspread, cried: 'Help, for God's sake, help!'
bent her head down as if to see Gregor better, yet on the contrary kept backing senselessly away; had quite forgotten that
the laden table stood behind her: sat upon it hastily, as if in
absence of mind, when she bumped into it; and seemed altogether unaware that the big coffee-pot beside her was upset and
pouring coffee in a flood over the carpet.

'Mother, Mother,' said Gregor in a low voice and looked up
at her. The chief clerk, for the moment, had quite slipped from
his mind; instead, he could not resist snapping his jaws together at the sight of the creaming coffee. That made his
mother scream again, she fled from the table and fell into the
arms of his father, who hastened to catch her. But Gregor had
now no time to spare for his parents; the chief clerk was already
on the stairs; with his chin on the banisters he was taking one
last backward look. Gregor made a spring, to be as sure as possible of overtaking him; the chief clerk must have divined his
intention, for he leapt down several steps and vanished; he was
still yelling 'Ugh!' and it echoed through the whole staircase.
Unfortunately, the flight of the chief clerk seemed completely
to upset Gregor's father, who had remained relatively calm
until now, for instead of running after the man himself, or at
least not hindering Gregor in his pursuit, he seized in his right
hand the walking-stick which the chief clerk had left behind on
a chair, together with a hat and great-coat, snatched in his left
hand a large newspaper from the table and began stamping his
feet and flourishing the stick and the newspaper to drive Gregor
back into his room. No entreaty of Gregor's availed, indeed no
entreaty was even understood, however humbly he bent his
head his father only stamped on the floor the more loudly. Behind his father his mother had torn open a window, despite the
cold weather, and was leaning far out of it with her face in her
hands. A strong draught set in from the street to the staircase,
the window curtains blew in, the newspapers on the table
fluttered, stray pages whisked over the floor. Pitilessly Gregor's

father drove him back, hissing and crying 'Shoo!' like a savage. But Gregor was quite unpractised in walking backwards, it really was a slow business. If he only had a chance to turn round he could get back to his room at once, but he was afraid of exasperating his father by the slowness of such a rotation and at any moment the stick in his father's hand might hit him a fatal blow on the back or on the head. In the end, however, nothing else was left for him to do since to his horror he observed that in moving backwards he could not even control the direction he took; and so, keeping an anxious eye on his father all the time over his shoulder, he began to turn round as quickly as he could, which was in reality very slowly. Perhaps his father noted his good intentions, for he did not interfere except every now and then to help him in the manoeuvre from a distance with the point of the stick. If only he would have stopped making that unbearable hissing noise! It made Gregor quite lose his head. He had turned almost completely round when the hissing noise so distracted him that he even turned a little the wrong way again. But when at last his head was fortunately right in front of the doorway, it appeared that his body was too broad simply to get through the opening. His father, of course, in his present mood was far from thinking of such a thing as opening the other half of the door, to let Gregor have enough space. He had merely the fixed idea of driving Gregor back into his room as quickly as possible. He would never have suffered Gregor to make the circumstantial preparations for standing up on end and perhaps slipping his way through the door. Maybe he was now making more noise than ever to urge Gregor forward, as if no obstacle impeded him; to Gregor, anyhow, the noise in his rear sounded no longer like the voice of one single father; this was really no joke, and Gregor thrust himself – come what might – into the doorway. One side of his body rose up, he was tilted at an angle in the doorway, his flank was quite bruised, horrid blotches stained the white door, soon he was stuck fast and, left to himself, could not have moved at all, his legs on one side fluttered trembling in the air, those on the other were crushed painfully to the floor – when from behind his father gave him a strong push which was literally a deliverance and he flew far into the room, bleeding freely. The door was slammed behind him with the stick, and then at last there was silence.

CHAPTER II

NOT until it was twilight did Gregor awake out of a deep sleep, more like a swoon than a sleep. He would certainly have wakened up of his own accord not much later, for he felt himself sufficiently rested and well-slept, but it seemed to him as if a fleeting step and a cautious shutting of the door leading into the hall had aroused him. The electric lights in the street cast a pale sheen here and there on the ceiling and the upper surfaces of the furniture, but down below, where he lay, it was dark. Slowly, awkwardly trying out his feelers, which he now first learned to appreciate, he pushed his way to the door to see what had been happening there. His left side felt like one single, long, unpleasantly tense scar, and he had actually to limp on his two rows of legs. One little leg, moreover, had been severely damaged in the course of that morning's events – it was almost a miracle that only one had been damaged – and trailed uselessly behind him.

He had reached the door before he discovered what had really drawn him to it: the smell of food. For there stood a basin filled with fresh milk in which floated little sops of white bread. He could almost have laughed with joy, since he was now still hungrier than in the morning, and he dipped his head almost over the eyes straight into the milk. But soon in disappointment he withdrew it again; not only did he find it difficult to feed because of his tender left side – and he could only feed with the palpitating collaboration of his whole body – he did not like the milk either, although milk had been his favourite drink and that was certainly why his sister had set it there for him, indeed it was almost with repulsion that he turned away from the basin and crawled back to the middle of the room.

He could see through the crack of the door that the gas was turned on in the living-room, but while usually at this time his father made a habit of reading the afternoon newspaper in a loud voice to his mother and occasionally to his sister as well, not a sound was now to be heard. Well, perhaps his father had recently given up this habit of reading aloud, which his sister had mentioned so often in conversation and in her letters. But there was the same silence all around, although the flat was certainly not empty of occupants. 'What a quiet life our family has been leading,' said Gregor to himself, and as he sat there motionless staring into the darkness he felt great pride in the fact that he had been able to provide such a life for his parents and sister in such a fine flat. But what if all the quiet, the comfort, the contentment were now to end in horror? To keep himself from being lost in such thoughts Gregor took refuge in movement and crawled up and down the room.

Once during the long evening one of the side-doors was opened a little and quickly shut again, later the other side-door too; someone had apparently wanted to come in and then thought better of it. Gregor now stationed himself immediately before the living-room door, determined to persuade any hesitating visitor to come in or at least to discover who it might be; but the door was not opened again and he waited in vain. In the early morning, when the doors were locked, they had all wanted to come in, now that he had opened one door and the other had apparently been opened during the day, no one came in and even the keys were on the other side of the doors.

It was late at night before the gas went out in the living-room, and Gregor could easily tell that his parents and his sister had all stayed awake until then, for he could clearly hear the three of them stealing away on tip-toe. No one was likely to visit him, not until the morning, that was certain; so he had plenty of time to meditate at his leisure on how he was to arrange his life afresh. But the lofty, empty room in which he had to lie flat on the floor filled him with an apprehension he could not account for, since it had been his very own room for the past five years and with a half unconscious action, not without a slight feeling of shame, he scuttled under the sofa, where he felt comfortable at once, although his back was a little cramped and he could not lift his head up, and his only regret was that his body was too broad to get the whole of it under the sofa.

He stayed there all night, spending the time partly in a light slumber, from which his hunger kept waking him up with a start, and partly in worrying and sketching vague hopes, which all led to the same conclusion, that he must lie low for the present and, by exercising patience and the utmost consideration, help the family to bear the inconvenience he was bound to cause them in his present condition.

Very early in the morning, it was still almost night, Gregor had the chance to test the strength of his new resolutions, for his sister, nearly fully dressed, opened the door from the hall and peered in. She did not see him at once, yet when she caught sight of him under the sofa – well, he had to be somewhere, he couldn't have flown away, could he? – she was so startled that without being able to help it she slammed the door shut again. But as if regretting her behaviour she opened the door again immediately and came in on tip-toe, as if she were visiting an invalid or even a stranger. Gregor had pushed his head forward to the very edge of the sofa and watched her. Would she notice that he had left the milk standing, and not for lack of hunger, and would she bring in some other kind of food more to his taste? If she did not do it of her own accord, he would rather starve than draw her attention to the fact, although he felt a wild impulse to dart out from under the sofa, throw himself at her feet and beg her for something to eat. But his sister at once noticed, with surprise, that the basin was still full, except for a little milk that had been spilt all round it, she lifted it immediately, not with her bare hands, true, but with a cloth and carried it away. Gregor was wildly curious to know what she would bring instead, and made various speculations about it. Yet what she actually did next, in the goodness of her heart, he could never have guessed at. To find out what he liked she brought him a whole selection of food, all set out on an old newspaper. There were old, half-decayed vegetables; bones from last night's supper covered with a white sauce that had thickened; some raisins and almonds; a piece of cheese that Gregor would have called uneatable two days ago; a dry roll of bread, a buttered roll, and a roll both buttered and salted. Besides all that, she set down again the same basin, into which she had poured some water, and which was apparently to be reserved for his exclusive use. And with fine tact, knowing that Gregor would not eat in her presence, she withdrew quickly and even turned the key, to let him understand that he could take his ease as much as he liked. Gregor's legs all whizzed towards the food. His wounds must have healed completely, moreover, for he felt no disability, which amazed him and made him reflect how more than a month ago he had cut one finger a little with a knife and had still suffered pain from the wound only the day before yesterday. Am I less sensitive now? he thought, and sucked greedily at the cheese, which above all the other edibles attracted him at once and strongly. One after another and with tears of satisfaction in his eyes he quickly devoured the cheese, the vegetables and the sauce; the fresh food, on the other hand, had no charms for him, he could not even stand the smell of it and actually dragged away to some little distance the things he could eat. He had long finished his meal and was only lying lazily on the same spot when his sister turned the key slowly as a sign for him to retreat. That roused him at once, although he was nearly asleep, and he hurried under the sofa again. But it took considerable self-control for him to stay under the sofa, even for the short time his sister was in the room, since the large meal had swollen his body somewhat and he was so cramped he could hardly breathe. Slight attacks of breathlessness afflicted him and his eyes were starting a little out of his head as he watched his unsuspecting sister sweeping together with a broom not only the remains of what he had eaten but even the things he had not touched, as if these were now of no use to anyone, and hastily shovelling it all into a bucket, which she covered with a wooden lid and carried away. Hardly had she turned her back when Gregor came from under the sofa and stretched and pulled himself out.

In this manner Gregor was fed, once in the early morning while his parents and the servant-girl were still asleep, and a second time after they had all had their midday dinner, for then his parents took a short nap and the servant-girl could be sent out on some errand or other by his sister. Not that they would have wanted him to starve, of course, but perhaps they could not have borne to know more about his feeding than from hearsay, perhaps, too, his sister wanted to spare them such little anxieties wherever possible, since they had quite enough to bear as it was.

Under what pretext the doctor and the locksmith had been got rid of on that first morning Gregor could not discover, for since what he said was not understood by the others it never struck any of them, not even his sister, that he could understand what they said, and so whenever his sister came into his room he had to content himself with hearing her utter only a sigh now and then and an occasional appeal to the saints. Later on, when she had got a little used to the situation – of course she could never get completely used to it – she sometimes threw out a remark which was kindly meant or could be so interpreted. 'Well, he liked his dinner today,' she would say when Gregor had made a good clearance of his food, and when he had not eaten, which gradually happened more and more often, she would say almost sadly: 'Everything's been left standing again.'

But although Gregor could get no news directly, he overheard a lot from the neighbouring rooms, and as soon as voices were

audible, he would run to the door of the room concerned and
press his whole body against it. In the first few days especially
there was no conversation that did not refer to him somehow,
even if only indirectly. For two whole days there were family
consultations at every mealtime about what should be done;
but also between meals the same subject was discussed, for there
were always at least two members of the family at home, since
no one wanted to be alone in the flat and to leave it quite empty
was unthinkable. And on the very first of these days the household cook – it was not quite clear what and how much she knew
of the situation – went down on her knees to his mother and
begged leave to go, and when she departed, a quarter of an hour
later, gave thanks for her dismissal with tears in her eyes as if
for the greatest benefit that could have been conferred on her,
and without any prompting swore a solemn oath that she
would never say a single word to anyone about what had
happened.

Now Gregor's sister had to cook too, helping her mother;
true, the cooking did not amount to much, for they ate scarcely
anything. Gregor was always hearing one of the family vainly
urging another to eat and getting no answer but: 'Thanks, I've
had all I want,' or something similar. Perhaps they drank nothing either. Time and again his sister kept asking his father if he
wouldn't like some beer and offered kindly to go and fetch it
herself, and when he made no answer suggested that she could
ask the concierge to fetch it, so that he need feel no sense of
obligation, but then a round 'No' came from his father and no
more was said about it.

In the course of that very first day Gregor's father explained
the family's financial position and prospects to both his mother
and his sister. Now and then he rose from the table to get some
voucher or memorandum out of the small safe he had rescued
from the collapse of his business five years earlier. One could
hear him opening the complicated lock and rustling papers out
and shutting it again. This statement made by his father was

the first cheerful information Gregor had heard since his imprisonment. He had been of the opinion that nothing at all was left over from his father's business, at least his father had never said anything to the contrary, and, of course, he had not asked him directly. At that time Gregor's sole desire was to do his utmost to help the family to forget as soon as possible the catastrophe which had overwhelmed the business and thrown them all into a state of complete despair. And so he had set to work with unusual ardour and almost overnight had become a commercial traveller instead of a little clerk, with, of course, much greater chances of earning money, and his success was immediately translated into good round coin which he could lay on the table for his amazed and happy family. These had been fine times, and they had never recurred, at least not with the same sense of glory, although later on Gregor had earned so much money that he was able to meet the expenses of the whole household and did so. They had simply got used to it, both the family and Gregor; the money was gratefully accepted and gladly given, but there was no special uprush of warm feeling. With his sister alone had he remained intimate, and it was a secret plan of his that she, who loved music, unlike himself, and could play movingly on the violin, should be sent next year to study at the Conservatorium, despite the great expense that would entail, which must be made up in some other way. During his brief visits home the Conservatorium was often mentioned in the talks he had with his sister, but always merely as a beautiful dream which could never come true, and his parents discouraged even these innocent references to it; yet Gregor had made up his mind firmly about it and meant to announce the fact with due solemnity on Christmas Day.

Such were the thoughts, completely futile in his present condition, that went through his head as he stood clinging upright to the door and listening. Sometimes out of sheer weariness he had to give up listening and let his head fall negligently against the door, but he always had to pull himself together again at once, for even the slight sound his head made was audible next door and brought all conversation to a stop. 'What can he be doing now?' his father would say after a while, obviously turning towards the door, and only then would the interrupted conversation gradually be set going again.

Gregor was now informed as amply as he could wish – for his father tended to repeat himself in his explanations, partly because it was a long time since he had handled such matters and partly because his mother could not always grasp things at once – that a certain amount of investments, a very small amount it was true, had survived the wreck of their fortunes and had even increased a little because the dividends had not been touched meanwhile. And besides that, the money Gregor brought home every month – he had kept only a few dollars for himself – had never been quite used up and now amounted to a small capital sum. Behind the door Gregor nodded his head eagerly, rejoiced at this evidence of unexpected thrift and foresight. True, he could really have paid off some more of his father's debts to the chief with this extra money, and so brought much nearer the day on which he could quit his job, but doubtless it was better the way his father had arranged it.

Yet this capital was by no means sufficient to let the family live on the interest of it; for one year, perhaps, or at the most two, they could live on the principal, that was all. It was simply a sum that ought not to be touched and should be kept for a rainy day; money for living expenses would have to be earned. Now his father was still hale enough but an old man, and he had done no work for the past five years and could not be expected to do much; during these five years, the first years of leisure in his laborious though unsuccessful life, he had grown rather fat and become sluggish. And Gregor's old mother, how was she to earn a living with her asthma, which troubled her even when she walked through the flat and kept her lying on a sofa every other day panting for breath beside an open window? And was his sister to earn her bread, she who was still a child of seventeen and whose life hitherto had been so pleasant, consisting as it did in dressing herself nicely, sleeping long, helping in the housekeeping, going out to a few modest entertainments, and above all playing the violin? At first, whenever the need for earning money was mentioned, Gregor let go his hold on the door and threw himself down on the cool leather sofa beside it, he felt so hot with shame and grief.

Often he just lay there the long nights through without sleeping at all, scrabbling for hours on the leather. Or he nerved himself to the great effort of pushing an arm-chair to the window, then crawled up over the window-sill and, braced against the chair, leaned against the window-panes, obviously in some recollection of the sense of freedom that looking out of a window always used to give him. For in reality, day by day, things that were even a little way off were growing dimmer to his sight; the hospital across the street, which he used to execrate for being all too often before his eyes, was now quite beyond his range of vision, and if he had not known that he lived in Charlotte Street, a quiet street but still a city street, he might have believed that his window gave on a desert waste where grey sky and grey land blended indistinguishably into each other. His quick-witted sister only needed to observe twice that the arm-chair stood by the window; after that, whenever she had tidied the room, she always pushed the chair back to the same place at the window and even left the inner casements open.

If he could have spoken to her and thanked her for all she had to do for him, he could have borne her ministrations better; as it was, they oppressed him. She certainly tried to make as light as possible of whatever was disagreeable in her task, and as time went on she succeeded, of course, more and more, but time brought more enlightenment to Gregor too. The very way she came in distressed him. Hardly was she in the room when she rushed to the window, without even taking time to shut the door, careful as she was usually to shield the sight of Gregor's room from the others, and, as if she were almost suffocating, tore the casements open with hasty fingers, standing then in the open draught for a while, even in the bitterest cold and drawing deep breaths. This noisy scurry of hers upset Gregor twice a day; he would crouch trembling under the sofa all the time, knowing quite well that she would certainly have spared him such a disturbance had she found it at all possible to stay in his presence without opening the window.

On one occasion, about a month after Gregor's metamorphosis, when there was surely no reason for her to be still startled at his appearance, she came a little earlier than usual and found him gazing out the window, quite motionless, and thus well placed to look like a bogey. Gregor would not have been surprised had she not come in at all, for she could not immediately open the window while he was there, but not only did she retreat, she jumped back as if in alarm and banged the door shut; a stranger might well have thought that he had been lying in wait for her there meaning to bite her. Of course he hid himself under the sofa at once, but he had to wait until midday before she came again, and she seemed more ill-at-ease than usual. This made him realize how repulsive the sight of him still was to her, and that it was bound to go on being repulsive, and what an effort it must cost her not to run away even from the sight of the small portion of his body that stuck out from under the sofa. In order to spare her that, therefore, one day he carried a sheet on his back to the sofa – it cost him four hours' labour – and arranged it there in such a way as to hide him completely, so that even if she were to bend down she could not see him. Had she considered the sheet unnecessary, she would certainly have stripped it off the sofa again, for it was clear enough that this curtaining and confining of himself was not likely to conduce to Gregor's comfort, but she left it where it was, and Gregor even fancied that he caught a thankful glance from her eye when he lifted the sheet carefully a very little with his head to see how she was taking the new arrangement.

For the first fortnight his parents could not bring themselves to the point of entering his room, and he often heard them expressing their appreciation of his sister's activities, whereas formerly they had frequently scolded her for being as they thought a somewhat useless daughter. But now, both of them often waited outside the door, his father and his mother, while his sister tidied his room, and as soon as she came out she had to tell them exactly how things were in the room, what Gregor had eaten, how he had conducted himself this time, and whether there was not perhaps some slight improvement in his condition. His mother, moreover, began relatively soon to want to visit him, but his father and sister dissuaded her at first with arguments which Gregor listened to very attentively and altogether approved. Later, however, she had to be held back by main force, and when she cried out: 'Do let me in to Gregor, he is my unfortunate son! Cannot you understand that I must go to him?' Gregor thought that it might be well to have her come in, not every day, of course, but perhaps once a week; she understood things, after all, much better than his sister, who was only a child despite the efforts she was making and had perhaps taken on so difficult a task merely out of childish thoughtlessness.

Gregor's desire to see his mother was soon fulfilled. During the daytime he did not want to show himself at the window, out of consideration for his parents, but he could not crawl very far around the few square yards of floor-space he had, nor could he bear lying quietly at rest all during the night, while he was fast losing any interest he had ever taken in food, so that for mere recreation he had formed the habit of crawling criss-cross over the walls and ceiling. He especially enjoyed hanging suspended from the ceiling; it was much better than lying on the floor; one could breathe more freely; one's body swung and rocked lightly; and in the almost blissful absorption induced by this suspension it could happen to his own surprise that he let go and fell plump on the floor. Yet he now had his body much better under control than formerly, and even such a big fall did him no harm. His sister at once remarked the new distraction Gregor had found for himself – he left traces behind him of the sticky stuff on his soles wherever he crawled – and she got the idea in her head of giving him as wide a field as possible to crawl in and of removing the pieces of furniture that hindered him, above all the chest of drawers and the writing-desk. But that was more than she could manage all by herself; she did not dare ask her father to help her; and as for the servant-girl, a young creature of sixteen who had had the courage to stay on after the cook's departure, she could not be asked to help, for she had begged as an especial favour that she might keep the kitchen door locked and open it only on a definite summons; so there was nothing left but to apply to her mother at an hour when her father was out. And the old lady did come, with exclamations of joyful eagerness, which, however, died away at the door of Gregor's room. Gregor's sister, of course, went in first, to see that everything was in order before letting his mother enter. In great haste Gregor pulled the sheet lower and rucked it more in folds so that it really looked as if it had been thrown accidentally over the sofa. And this time he did not peer out from under it; he renounced the pleasure of seeing his mother on this occasion and was only glad that she had come at all. 'Come in, he's out of sight,' said his sister, obviously leading her mother in by the hand. Gregor could now hear the two women struggling to shift the heavy old chest from its place, and his sister claiming the greater part of the labour for herself, without listening to the admonitions of her mother who feared she might overstrain herself. It took a long time. After at least a quarter of an hour's tugging his mother objected that the chest had better be left where it was, for in the first place it was too heavy and could never be got out before his father came home, and standing in the middle of the room like that it would only hamper Gregor's movements, while in the second place it was not at all certain that removing the furniture would be doing a service to Gregor. She was inclined to think to the contrary; the sight of the naked walls made her own heart heavy, and why shouldn't Gregor have the same feeling, considering that he had been used to his furniture for so long and might well feel forlorn without it. 'And doesn't it look,' she concluded in a low voice – in fact she had been almost whispering all the time as if to avoid letting Gregor, whose exact whereabouts she did not know, hear even the tones of her voice, for she was convinced that he could not understand her words – 'doesn't it look as if we were showing him, by taking away his furniture, that we have given up hope of his ever getting better and are just leaving him coldly to himself? I think it would be best to keep his room exactly as it has always been, so that when he comes back to us he will find everything unchanged and be able all the more easily to forget what has happened in between.' On hearing these words from his mother Gregor realized that the lack of all direct human speech for the past two months together with the monotony of family life must have confused his mind, otherwise he could not account for the fact that he had quite earnestly looked forward to having his room emptied of furnishing. Did he really want his warm room, so comfortably fitted with old family furniture, to be turned into a naked den in which he would certainly be able to crawl unhampered in all directions but at the price of shedding simultaneously all recollection of his human background? He had indeed been so near the brink of forgetfulness that only the voice of his mother, which he had not heard for so long, had drawn him back from it. Nothing should be taken out of his room; everything must stay as it was; he could not dispense with the good influence of the furniture on his state of mind; and even if the furniture did hamper him in his senseless crawling round and round, that was no drawback but a great advantage.

Unfortunately his sister was of the contrary opinion; she had grown accustomed, and not without reason, to consider herself an expert in Gregor's affairs as against her parents, and so her mother's advice was now enough to make her determined on the removal not only of the chest and the writing-desk, which had been her first intention, but of all the furniture except the indispensable sofa. This determination was not, of course, merely the outcome of childish recalcitrance and of the self-confidence she had recently developed so unexpectedly and at such cost; she had in fact perceived that Gregor needed a lot of space to crawl about in, while on the other hand he never used the furniture at all, so far as could be seen. Another factor might also have been the enthusiastic temperament of an adolescent girl, which seeks to indulge itself on every opportunity and which now tempted Grete to exaggerate the horror of her brother's circumstances in order that she might do all the more for him. In a room where Gregor lorded it all alone over empty walls no one save herself was likely ever to set foot.

And so she was not to be moved from her resolve by her mother, who seemed moreover to be ill-at-ease in Gregor's room and therefore unsure of herself, was soon reduced to silence and helped her daughter as best she could to push the chest outside. Now, Gregor could do without the chest, if need be, but the writing-desk he must retain. As soon as the two women had got the chest out of his room, groaning as they pushed it, Gregor stuck his head out from under the sofa to see how he might intervene as kindly and cautiously as possible. But as bad luck would have it, his mother was the first to return, leaving Grete clasping the chest in the room next door where she was trying to shift it all by herself, without of course moving it from the spot. His mother, however, was not accustomed to the sight of him, it might sicken her, and so in alarm Gregor backed quickly to the other end of the sofa, yet could not prevent the sheet from swaying a little in front. That was enough to put her on the alert. She paused, stood still for a moment, and then went back to Grete.

Although Gregor kept reassuring himself that nothing out of the way was happening, that only a few bits of furniture were being changed round, he soon had to admit that all this trotting to and fro of the two women, their little ejaculations, and the scraping of furniture along the floor affected him like a vast disturbance coming from all sides at once, and however much he tucked his head and legs and cowered to the very floor he was bound to confess that he would not be able to stand it for long. They were clearing his room out; taking away everything he loved; the chest in which he kept his fret-saw and other tools was already dragged off; they were now loosening the writing-desk which had almost sunk into the floor; the desk at which he had done all his homework when he was at the commercial academy, at the grammar school – he had no more time to waste in weighing the good intentions of the two women, whose existence he had by now almost forgotten, for they were so exhausted that they were labouring in silence and nothing could be heard but the heavy scuffling of their feet.

And so he rushed out – the women were just leaning against the writing-desk in the next room to give themselves a breather – and four times changed his direction, since he really did not know what to rescue first, then on the wall opposite, which was already otherwise cleared, he was struck by the picture of the lady muffled in so much fur and quickly crawled up to it and pressed himself to the glass, which was a good surface to hold on to and comforted his hot belly. This picture at least, which was entirely hidden beneath him, was going to be removed by no-body. He turned his head towards the door of the living-room so as to observe the women when they came back.

They had not allowed themselves much of a rest and were already coming; Grete had twined her arm round her mother and was almost supporting her. 'Well, what shall we take now?' said Grete, looking round. Her eyes met Gregor's from the wall. She kept her composure, presumably because of her mother, bent her head down to her mother, to keep her from looking up, and said, although in a fluttering, unpremeditated voice: 'Come, hadn't we better go back to the living-room for a moment?' Her intentions were clear enough to Gregor, she wanted to bestow her mother in safety and then chase him down from the wall. Well, just let her try it! He clung to his picture and would not give it up. He would rather fly in Grete's face.

But Grete's words had succeeded in disquieting her mother, who took a step to one side, caught sight of the huge brown mass on the flowered wallpaper, and before she was really conscious that what she saw was Gregor, screamed in a loud, hoarse voice: 'Oh God, oh God!', fell with outspread arms over the sofa as if giving up the ghost and did not move.'Gregor!' cried his sister, shaking her fist and glaring at him. This was the first time she had directly addressed him since his metamorphosis. She ran into the next room for some aromatic essence with which to rouse her mother from her fainting fit. Gregor wanted to help too – there was still time to rescue the picture – but he was stuck fast to the glass and had to tear himself loose; he then ran after his sister into the next room as if he could advise her, as he used to do; but then had to stand helpless behind her; she meanwhile searched among various small bottles and when she turned round startled in alarm at the sight of him; one bottle fell on the floor and broke; a splinter of glass cut Gregor's face and some kind of corrosive medicine splashed him; without pausing a moment longer Grete gathered up all the bottles she could carry and ran to her mother with them; she banged the door shut with her foot. Gregor was now cut off from his mother, who was perhaps nearly dying because of him; he dared not open the door for fear of frightening away his sister, who had to stay with her mother; there was nothing he could do but wait; and harassed by self-reproach and worry he began now to crawl to and fro over everything, walls, furniture and ceiling, and finally in his despair, when the whole room seemed to be reeling round him, fell down on to the middle of the big table.

A little while elapsed, Gregor was still lying there feebly and all around was quiet, perhaps that was a good omen. Then the door-bell rang. The servant-girl was of course locked in her kitchen, and Grete would have to open the door. It was his father. 'What's been happening?' were his first words; Grete's face must have told him everything. Grete answered in a muffled voice, apparently hiding her head on his breast: 'Mother has been fainting, but she's better now. Gregor's broken loose.' 'Just what I expected,' said his father, 'just what I've been telling you, but you women would never listen.' It was clear to Gregor that his father had taken the worst interpretation of Grete's all too brief statement and was assuming that Gregor had been guilty of some violent act. Therefore Gregor must now try to propitiate his father, since he had neither time nor means for an explanation. And so he fled to the door of his own room and crouched against it, to let his father see as soon as he came in from the hall that his son had the good intention of getting back into his room immediately and that it was not necessary to drive him there, but that if only the door were opened he would disappear at once.

Yet his father was not in the mood to perceive such fine distinctions: 'Ah!' he cried as soon as he appeared, in a tone which sounded at once angry and exultant. Gregor drew his head back from the door and lifted it to look at his father. Truly, this was not the father he had imagined to himself; admittedly he had been too absorbed of late in his new recreation of crawling over the ceiling to take the same interest as before in what was happening elsewhere in the flat, and he ought really to be prepared for some changes. And yet, and yet, could that be his father? The man who used to lie wearily sunk in bed whenever Gregor set out on a business journey; who welcomed him back of an evening lying in a long chair in a dressing-gown; who could not really rise to his feet but only lifted his arms in greeting, and on the rare occasions when he did go out with his family, on one or two Sundays a year and on high holidays, walked between Gregor and his mother, who were slow walkers anyhow, even more slowly than they did, muffled in his old great-coat, shuffling laboriously forward with the help of his crook-handled stick which he set down most cautiously at every step and, whenever he wanted to say anything, nearly always came to a full stop and gathered his escort around him? Now he was standing there in fine shape; dressed in a smart blue uniform with gold buttons, such as bank messengers wear; his strong double chin bulged over the stiff high collar of his jacket; from under his bushy eyebrows his black eyes darted fresh and penetrating glances; his one-time tangled white hair had been combed flat on either side of a shining and carefully exact parting. He pitched his cap, which bore a gold monogram – probably the badge of some bank – in a wide sweep across the whole room on to a sofa, and with the tail-ends of his jacket thrown back, his hands in his trouser pockets, advanced with a grim visage towards Gregor. Likely enough he did not himself know what he meant to do; at any rate he lifted his feet uncommonly high, and Gregor was dumbfounded at the enormous size of his shoe soles. But Gregor could not risk standing up to him, aware as he had been from the very first day of his new life that his father believed only the severest measures suitable for dealing with him. And so he ran before his father, stopping when he stopped and scuttling forward again when his father made any kind of move. In this way they circled the room several times without anything decisive happening, indeed the whole operation did not even look like a pursuit because it was carried out so slowly. And so Gregor did not leave the floor, for he feared that his father might take as a piece of peculiar wickedness any excursion of his over the walls or the ceiling. All the same, he could not stay this course much longer, for while his father took one step he had to carry out a whole series of movements. He was already beginning to feel breathless, just as in his former life his lungs had not been very dependable. As he was staggering along, trying to concentrate his energy on running, hardly keeping his eyes open; in his dazed state never even thinking of any other escape than simply going forward; and having almost forgotten that the walls were free to him, which in this room were well provided with finely carved pieces of furniture full of knobs and crevices – suddenly something lightly flung landed close behind him and rolled before him. It was an apple; a second apple followed immediately; Gregor came to a stop in alarm; there was no point in running on, for his father was determined to bombard him. He had filled his pockets with fruit from the dish on the sideboard and was now shying apple after apple, without taking particularly good aim for the moment. The small red apples rolled about the floor as if magnetized and cannoned into each other. An apple thrown without much force grazed Gregor's back and glanced off harmlessly. But another following immediately landed right on his back and sank in; Gregor wanted to drag himself forward, as if this startling, incredible pain could be left behind him; but he felt as if nailed to the spot and flattened himself out in a complete derangement of all his senses. With his last conscious look he saw the door of his room being torn open and his mother rushing out ahead of his screaming sister, in her under-bodice, for her daughter had loosened her clothing to let her breathe more freely and recover from her swoon, he saw his mother rushing towards his father, leaving one after another behind her on the floor her loosened petticoats, stumbling over her petticoats straight to his father and embracing him, in complete union with him – but here Gregor's sight began to fail – with her hands clasped round his father's neck as she begged for her son's life.

CHAPTER III

The serious injury done to Gregor, which disabled him for more than a month – the apple went on sticking in his body as a visible reminder since no one ventured to remove it – seemed to have made even his father recollect that Gregor was a member of the family, despite his present unfortunate and repulsive shape, and ought not to be treated as an enemy, that, on the contrary, family duty required the suppression of disgust and the exercise of patience, nothing but patience.

And although his injury had impaired, probably for ever, his powers of movement, and for the time being it took him long, long minutes to creep across his room like an old invalid – there was no question now of crawling up the wall – yet in his own opinion he was sufficiently compensated for this worsening of his condition by the fact that towards evening the living-room door, which he used to watch intently for an hour or two before-hand, was always thrown open, so that lying in the darkness of his room, invisible to the family, he could see them all at the lamp-lit table and listen to their talk, by general consent as it were, very different from his earlier eavesdropping.

True, their intercourse lacked the lively character of former times, which he had always called to mind with a certain wist-fulness in the small hotel bedrooms where he had been wont to throw himself down, tired out, on damp bedding. They were now mostly very silent. Soon after supper his father would fall asleep in his arm-chair; his mother and sister would admonish one another to be silent; his mother, bending low over the lamp, stitched at fine sewing for an underwear firm; his sister, who had taken a job as a sales-girl, was learning shorthand and French in the evenings on the chance of bettering herself. Sometimes his father woke up, and as if quite unaware that he had been sleeping said to his mother: 'What a lot of sewing you're doing today!' and at once fell asleep again, while the two women exchanged a tired smile.

With a kind of mulishness his father persisted in keeping his uniform on even in the house; his dressing-gown hung uselessly on its peg and he slept fully dressed where he sat, as if he were ready for service at any moment and even here only at the beck and call of his superior. As a result, his uniform, which was not brand new to start with, began to look dirty, despite all the loving care of the mother and sister to keep it clean, and Gregor often spent whole evenings gazing at the many greasy spots on the garment, gleaming with gold buttons always in a high state of polish, in which the old man sat sleeping in extreme discomfort and yet quite peacefully.

As soon as the clock struck ten his mother tried to rouse his father with gentle words and to persuade him after that to get into bed, for sitting there he could not have a proper sleep and that was what he needed most, since he had to go on duty at six. But with the mulishness that had obsessed him since he became a bank messenger he always insisted on staying longer at the table, although he regularly fell asleep again and in the end only with the greatest trouble could be got out of his arm-chair and into his bed. However insistently Gregor's mother and sister kept urging him with gentle reminders, he would go on slowly shaking his head for a quarter of an hour, keeping his eyes shut, and refuse to get to his feet. The mother plucked at his sleeve, whispering endearments in his ear, the sister left her lessons to come to her mother's help, but Gregor's father was not to be caught. He would only sink down deeper in his chair. Not until the two women hoisted him up by the armpits did he open his eyes and look at them both, one after the other, usually with the remark: 'This is a life. This is the peace and quiet of my old age.' And leaning on the two of them he would heave himself up, with difficulty, as if he were a great burden to himself, suffer them to lead him as far as the door and then wave them off and go on alone, while the mother abandoned her needlework and the sister her pen in order to run after him and help him farther.

Who could find time, in this overworked and tired-out family, to bother about Gregor more than was absolutely needful? The household was reduced more and more; the servant-girl was turned off; a gigantic bony charwoman with white hair flying round her head came in morning and evening to do the rough work; everything else was done by Gregor's mother, as well as great piles of sewing. Even various family ornaments, which his mother and sister used to wear with pride at parties and celebrations, had to be sold, as Gregor discovered of an evening from hearing them all discuss the prices obtained. But what they lamented most was the fact that they could not leave the flat which was now much too big for their present circumstances, because they could not think of any way to shift Gregor. Yet Gregor saw well enough that consideration for him was not the main difficulty preventing the removal, for they could have easily shifted him in some suitable box with a few air-holes in it; what really kept them from moving into another flat was rather their own complete hopelessness and the belief that they had been singled out for a misfortune such as had never happened to any of their relations or acquaintances. They fulfilled to the uttermost all that the world demands of poor people, the father fetched breakfast for the small clerks in the bank, the mother devoted her energy to making underwear for strangers, the sister trotted to and fro behind the counter at the behest of customers, but more than that they had not the strength to do. And the wound in Gregor's back began to nag at him afresh when his mother and sister, after getting his father into bed, came back again, left their work lying, drew close to each other and sat cheek by cheek; when his mother, pointing towards his room, said: 'Shut that door now, Grete,' and he was left again in darkness, while next door the women mingled their tears or perhaps sat dry-eyed staring at the table.

Gregor hardly slept at all by night or by day. He was often haunted by the idea that next time the door opened he would take the family's affairs in hand again just as he used to do; once more, after this long interval, there appeared in his thoughts the figures of the chief and the chief clerk, the commercial travellers and the apprentices, the porter who was so dull-witted, two or three friends in other firms, a chambermaid in one of the rural hotels, a sweet and fleeting memory, a cashier in a milliner's shop, whom he had wooed earnestly but too slowly – they all appeared, together with strangers or people he had quite forgotten, but instead of helping him and his family they were one and all unapproachable and he was glad when they vanished. At other times he would not be in the mood to bother about his family, he was only filled with rage at the way they were neglecting him, and although he had no clear idea of what he might care to eat he would make plans for getting into the larder to take the food that was after all his due, even if he were not hungry. His sister no longer took thought to bring him what might especially please him, but in the morning and at noon, before she went to business, hurriedly pushed into his room with her foot any food that was available, and in the evening cleared it out again with one sweep of the broom, heedless of whether it had been merely tasted, or – as most frequently happened – left untouched. The cleaning of his room, which she now did always in the evenings, could not have been more hastily done. Streaks of dirt stretched along the walls, here and there lay balls of dust and filth. At first Gregor used to station himself in some particularly filthy corner when his sister arrived, in order to reproach her with it, so to speak. But he could have sat there for weeks without getting her to make any improvement; she could see the dust as well as he did, but she had simply made up her mind to leave it alone. And yet, with a touchiness that was new to her, which seemed anyhow to have infected the whole family, she jealously guarded her claim to be the sole caretaker of Gregor's room. His mother once subjected his room to a thorough cleaning, which was achieved only by means of several buckets of water – all this dampness of course upset Gregor too and he lay widespread, sulky and motionless on the sofa – but she was well punished for it. Hardly had his sister noticed the changed aspect of his room that evening than she rushed in high dudgeon into the living-room and, despite the imploringly raised hands of her mother, burst into a storm of weeping, while her parents – her father had of course been startled out of his chair – looked on at first in helpless amazement; they, too, began to go into action; the father reproached the mother on his right for not having left the cleaning of Gregor's room to his sister; shrieked at the sister on his left that never again was she to be allowed to clean Gregor's room; while the mother tried to pull the father into his bedroom, since he was beyond himself with agitation; the sister, shaken with sobs, then beat upon the table with her small fists; and Gregor hissed loudly with rage because not one of them thought of shutting the door to spare him such a spectacle and so much noise.

Still, even if the sister, exhausted by her daily work, had grown tired of looking after Gregor as she did formerly, there was no need for his mother's intervention or for Gregor's being neglected at all. The charwoman was there. This old widow, whose strong bony frame had enabled her to survive the worst a long life could offer, by no means recoiled from Gregor. Without being in the least curious she had once by chance opened the door of his room and at the sight of Gregor, who, taken by surprise, began to rush to and fro although no one was chasing him, merely stood there with her arms folded. From that time she never failed to open his door a little for a moment, morning and evening, to have a look at him. At first she even used to call him to her with words which apparently she took to be friendly, such as: 'Come along, then, you old dung-beetle!' or 'Look at the old dung-beetle, then!' To such allocutions Gregor made no answer, but stayed motionless where he was, as if the door had never been opened. Instead of being allowed to disturb him so senselessly whenever the whim took her, she should rather have been ordered to clean out his room daily, that charwoman! Once, early in the morning – heavy rain was lashing on the window-panes, perhaps a sign that spring was on the way – Gregor was so exasperated when she began addressing him again that he ran at her, as if to attack her, although slowly and feebly enough. But the charwoman instead of showing fright merely lifted high a chair that happened to be beside the door, and as she stood there with her mouth wide open it was clear that she meant to shut it only when she brought the chair down on Gregor's back. 'So you're not coming any nearer?' she asked, as Gregor turned away again, and quietly put the chair back into the corner.

Gregor was now eating hardly anything. Only when he happened to pass the food laid out for him did he take a bit of something in his mouth as a pastime, kept it there for an hour at a time and usually spat it out again. At first he thought it was chagrin over the state of his room that prevented him from eating, yet he soon got used to the various changes in his room. It had become a habit in the family to push into his room things there was no room for elsewhere, and there were plenty of these now, since one of the rooms had been let to three lodgers. These serious young men – all three of them with full beards, as Gregor once observed through a crack in the door – had a passion for order, not only in their own room but, since they were now members of the household, in all its arrangements, especially in the kitchen. Superfluous, not to say dirty, objects they could not bear. Besides, they had brought with them most of the furnishings they needed. For this reason many things could be dispensed with that it was no use trying to sell but that should not be thrown away either. All of them found their way into Gregor's room. The ash-can likewise and the kitchen garbage-can. Anything that was not needed for the moment was simply flung into Gregor's room by the charwoman, who did everything in a hurry; fortunately Gregor usually saw only the object, whatever it was, and the hand that held it. Perhaps she intended to take the things away again as time and opportunity offered, or to collect them until she could throw them all out in a heap, but in fact they just lay wherever she happened to throw them, except when Gregor pushed his way through the junk-heap and shifted it somewhat, at first out of necessity, because he had not room enough to crawl, but later with increasing enjoyment, although after such excursions, being sad and weary to death, he would lie motionless for hours. And since the lodgers often ate their supper at home in the common living-room, the living-room door stayed shut many an evening, yet Gregor reconciled himself quite easily to the shutting of the door, for often enough on evenings when it was opened he had disregarded it entirely and lain in the darkest corner of his room, quite unnoticed by the family. But on one occasion the charwoman left the door open a little and it stayed ajar even when the lodgers came in for supper and the lamp was lit. They set themselves at the top end of the table where formerly Gregor and his father and mother had eaten their meals, unfolded their napkins and took knife and fork in hand. At once his mother appeared in the other doorway with a dish of meat and close behind her his sister with a dish of potatoes piled high. The food steamed with a thick vapour. The lodgers bent over the food set before them as if to scrutinize it before eating, in fact the man in the middle, who seemed to pass for an authority with the other two, cut a piece of meat as it lay on the dish, obviously to discover if it were tender or should be sent back to the kitchen. He showed satisfaction, and Gregor's mother and sister, who had been watching anxiously, breathed freely and began to smile.

The family itself took its meals in the kitchen. None the less, Gregor's father came into the living-room before going into the kitchen and with one prolonged bow, cap in hand, made a round of the table. The lodgers all stood up and murmured something in their beards. When they were alone again they ate their food in almost complete silence. It seemed remarkable to Gregor that among the various noises coming from the table he could always distinguish the sound of their masticating teeth, as if this were a sign to Gregor that one needed teeth, in order to eat, and that with toothless jaws even of the finest make one could do nothing. 'I'm hungry enough,' said Gregor sadly to himself, 'but not for that kind of food. How these lodgers are stuffing themselves, and here am I dying of starvation!'

On that very evening – during the whole of his time there

Gregor could not remember ever having heard the violin – the sound of violin-playing came from the kitchen. The lodgers had already finished their supper, the one in the middle had brought out a newspaper and given the other two a page apiece, and now they were leaning back at ease reading and smoking. When the violin began to play they pricked up their ears, got to their feet, and went on tip-toe to the hall door where they stood huddled together. Their movements must have been heard in the kitchen, for Gregor's father called out: 'Is the violin-playing disturbing you, gentlemen? It can be stopped at once.' 'On the contrary,' said the middle lodger, 'could not Fräulein Samsa come and play in this room, beside us, where it is much more convenient and comfortable?' 'Oh certainly,' cried Gregor's father, as if he were the violin-player. The lodgers came back into the living-room and waited. Presently Gregor's father arrived with the music-stand, his mother carrying the music and his sister with the violin. His sister quietly made everything ready to start playing; his parents, who had never let rooms before and so had an exaggerated idea of the courtesy due to lodgers, did not venture to sit down on their own chairs; his father leaned against the door, the right hand thrust between two buttons of his livery-coat, which was formally buttoned up; but his mother was offered a chair by one of the lodgers and, since she left the chair just where he had happened to put it, sat down in a corner to one side.

Gregor's sister began to play; the father and mother, from either side, intently watched the movements of her hands. Gregor, attracted by the playing, ventured to move forward a little until his head was actually inside the living-room. He felt hardly any surprise at his growing lack of consideration for the others; there had been a time when he prided himself on being considerate. And yet just on this occasion he had more reason than ever to hide himself, since owing to the amount of dust which lay thick in his room and rose into the air at the slightest movement, he, too, was covered with dust; fluff and hair and remnants of food trailed with him, caught on his back and along his sides; his indifference to everything was much too great for him to turn on his back and scrape himself clean on the carpet, as once he had done several times a day. And in spite of his condition, no shame deterred him from advancing a little over the spotless floor of the living-room.

To be sure, no one was aware of him. The family was entirely absorbed in the violin-playing; the lodgers, however, who first of all had stationed themselves, hands in pockets, much too close behind the music-stand so that they could all have read the music – which must have bothered his sister – had soon retreated to the window, half-whispering with down-bent heads, and stayed there while his father turned an anxious eye on them. Indeed, they were making it more than obvious that they had been disappointed in their expectation of hearing good or enjoyable violin-playing, that they had had more than enough of the performance and only out of courtesy suffered a continued disturbance of their peace. From the way they all kept blowing the smoke of their cigars high in the air through nose and mouth one could divine their irritation. And yet Gregor's sister was playing so beautifully. Her face leaned sideways, intently and sadly her eyes followed the notes of music. Gregor crawled a little farther forward and lowered his head to the ground so that it might be possible for his eyes to meet hers. Was he an animal, when music had such an effect upon him? He felt as if the way were opening before him to the unknown nourishment he craved. He was determined to push forward till he reached his sister, to pull at her skirt and so let her know that she was to come into his room with her violin, for no one here appreciated her playing as he would appreciate it. He would never let her out of his room, at least, not so long as he lived; his frightful appearance would become, for the first time, useful to him; he would watch all the doors of his room at once and spit at intruders; but his sister should need no constraint, she should stay with him of her own free will; she should sit beside

him on the sofa, bend down her ear to him and hear him confide that he had had the firm intention of sending her to the
Conservatorium, and that, but for his mishap, last Christmas –
surely Christmas was long past? – he would have announced it
to everybody without allowing a single objection. After this
confession his sister would be so touched that she would burst
into tears, and Gregor would then raise himself to her shoulder
and kiss her on the neck, which, now that she went to business
she kept free of any ribbon or collar.

'Mr Samsa!' cried the middle lodger to Gregor's father, and
pointed, without wasting any more words, at Gregor, now
working himself slowly forwards. The violin fell silent, the middle lodger first smiled to his friends with a shake of the head and
then looked at Gregor again. Instead of driving Gregor out, his
father seemed to think it more needful to begin by soothing
down the lodgers, although they were not at all agitated and
apparently found Gregor more entertaining than the violin-
playing. He hurried towards them and, spreading out his arms,
tried to urge them back into their own room and at the same
time to block their view of Gregor. They now began to be really
a little angry, one could not tell whether because of the old
man's behaviour or because it had just dawned on them that
all unwittingly they had such a neighbour as Gregor next door.
They demanded explanations of his father, they waved their
arms like him, tugged uneasily at their beards, and only with
reluctance backed towards their room. Meanwhile Gregor's
sister, who stood there as if lost when her playing was so
abruptly broken off, came to life again, pulled herself together
all at once after standing for a while holding violin and bow in
nervelessly hanging hands and staring at her music, pushed her
violin into the lap of her mother, who was still sitting in her
chair fighting asthmatically for breath, and ran into the lodgers'
room to which they were now being shepherded by her father
rather more quickly than before. One could see the pillows and
blankets on the beds flying under her accustomed fingers and

being laid in order. Before the lodgers had actually reached their room she had finished making the beds and slipped out.

The old man seemed once more to be so possessed by his mulish self-assertiveness that he was forgetting all the respect he should show to his lodgers. He kept driving them on and driving them on until in the very door of the bedroom the middle lodger stamped his foot loudly on the floor and so brought him to a halt. 'I beg to announce,' said the lodger, lifting one hand and looking also at Gregor's mother and sister, 'that because of the disgusting conditions prevailing in this household and family' – here he spat on the floor with emphatic brevity – 'I give you notice on the spot. Naturally I won't pay you a penny, not even for the days I have lived here, on the contrary, I shall consider bringing an action for damages against you, based on claims – believe me – that will be easily susceptible of proof.' He ceased and stared straight in front of him, as if he expected something. In fact his two friends at once rushed into the breach with these words: 'And we, too, give notice on the spot.' On that he seized the door-handle and shut the door with a slam.

Gregor's father, groping with his hands, staggered forward and fell into his chair; it looked as if he were stretching himself there for an ordinary evening nap, but the marked jerkings of his head, which was as if uncontrollable, showed that he was far from asleep. Gregor had simply stayed quietly all the time on the spot where the lodgers had espied him. Disappointment at the failure of his plan, perhaps also the weakness arising from extreme hunger, made it impossible for him to move. He feared, with a fair degree of certainty, that at any moment the general tension would discharge itself in a combined attack upon him, and he lay waiting. He did not react even to the noise made by the violin as it fell off his mother's lap from under her trembling fingers and gave out a resonant note.

'My dear parents,' said his sister, slapping her hand on the table by way of introduction, 'things can't go on like this. Perhaps you don't realize that, but I do. I won't utter my brother's name in the presence of this creature, and so all I say is: we must try to get rid of it. We've tried to look after it and to put up with it as far as is humanly possible, and I don't think anyone could reproach us in the slightest.'

'She is more than right,' said Gregor's father to himself. His mother, who was still choking for lack of breath, began to cough hollowly into her hand with a wild look in her eyes.

His sister rushed over to her and held her forehead. His father's thoughts seemed to have lost their vagueness at Grete's words, he sat more upright, fingering his service cap that lay among the plates still lying on the table from the lodgers' supper, and from time to time looked at the still form of Gregor.

'We must try to get rid of it,' his sister now said explicitly to her father, since her mother was coughing too much to hear a word, 'it will be the death of both of you, I can see that coming. When one has to work as hard as we do, all of us, one can't stand this continual torment at home on top of it. At least I can't stand it any longer.' And she burst into such a passion of sobbing that her tears dropped on her mother's face, where she wiped them off mechanically.

'My dear,' said the old man sympathetically, and with evident understanding, 'but what can we do?'

Gregor's sister merely shrugged her shoulders to indicate the feeling of helplessness that had now over-mastered her during her weeping fit, in contrast to her former confidence.

'If he could understand us,' said her father, half questioningly; Grete, still sobbing, vehemently waved a hand to show how unthinkable that was.

'If he could understand us,' repeated the old man, shutting his eyes to consider his daughter's conviction that understanding was impossible, 'then perhaps we might come to some agreement with him. But as it is — '

'He must go,' cried Gregor's sister, 'that's the only solution, Father. You must just try to get rid of the idea that this is

Gregor. The fact that we've believed it for so long is the root of all our trouble. But how can it be Gregor? If this were Gregor, he would have realized long ago that human beings can't live with such a creature, and he'd have gone away of his own accord. Then we wouldn't have any brother, but we'd be able to go on living and keep his memory in honour. As it is, this creature persecutes us, drives away our lodgers, obviously wants the whole apartment to himself and would have us all sleep in the gutter. Just look, Father,' she shrieked all at once, 'he's at it again!' And in an access of panic that was quite incomprehensible to Gregor she even quitted her mother, literally thrusting the chair from her as if she would rather sacrifice her mother than stay so near to Gregor, and rushed behind her father, who also rose up, being simply upset by her agitation, and half spread his arms out as if to protect her.

Yet Gregor had not the slightest intention of frightening anyone, far less his sister. He had only begun to turn round in order to crawl back to his room, but it was certainly a startling operation to watch, since because of his disabled condition he could not execute the difficult turning movements, except by lifting his head and then bracing it against the floor over and over again. He paused and looked round. His good intentions seemed to have been recognized; the alarm had only been momentary. Now they were all watching him in melancholy silence. His mother lay in her chair, her legs stiffly outstretched and pressed together, her eyes almost closing for sheer weariness; his father and his sister were sitting beside each other, his sister's arm around the old man's neck.

Perhaps I can go on turning round now, thought Gregor, and began his labours again. He could not stop himself from panting with the effort, and had to pause now and then to take breath. Nor did anyone harass him, he was left entirely to himself. When he had completed the turn-round he began at once to crawl straight back. He was amazed at the distance separating him from his room and could not understand how in his weak state he had managed to accomplish the same journey so recently, almost without remarking it. Intent on crawling as fast as possible, he barely noticed that not a single word, not an ejaculation from his family, interfered with his progress. Only when he was already in the doorway did he turn his head round, not completely, for his neck muscles were getting stiff, but enough to see that nothing had changed behind him except that his sister had risen to her feet. His last glance fell on his mother, who was now quite overcome by sleep.

Hardly was he well inside his room when the door was hastily pushed shut, bolted and locked. The sudden noise in his rear startled him so much that his little legs gave beneath him. It was his sister who had shown such haste. She had been standing ready waiting and had made a light spring forward, Gregor had not even heard her coming, and she cried 'At last!' to her parents as she turned the key in the lock.

'And what now?' said Gregor to himself, looking round in the darkness. Soon he made the discovery that he was now unable to stir a limb. This did not surprise him, rather it seemed unnatural that he should ever actually have been able to move on these feeble little legs. Otherwise he felt relatively comfortable. True, his whole body was aching, but it seemed that the pain was gradually growing less and would finally pass away. The rotting apple in his back and the inflamed path around it, all covered with soft dust, already hardly troubled him. He thought of his family with tenderness and love. The decision that he must disappear was one that he held to even more strongly than his sister – if that were possible. In this state of vacant and peaceful meditation he remained until the tower clock struck three in the morning. The first broadening of light in the world outside the window entered his consciousness once more. Then his head sank to the floor of its own accord and from his nostrils came the last faint flicker of his breath.

When the charwoman arrived early in the morning – what between her strength and her impatience she slammed all the doors so loudly, never mind how often she had been begged not to do so, that no one in the whole apartment could enjoy any quiet sleep after her arrival – she noticed nothing unusual as she took her customary peep into Gregor's room. She thought he was lying motionless on purpose, pretending to be in the sulks; she credited him with every kind of intelligence. Since she happened to have the long-handled broom in her hand she tried to tickle him up with it from the doorway. When that too produced no reaction she felt provoked and poked at him a little harder, and only when she had pushed him along the floor without meeting any resistance was her attention aroused. It did not take her long to establish the truth of the matter, and her eyes widened, she let out a whistle, yet did not waste much time over it but tore open the door of the Samsas' bedroom and yelled into the darkness at the top of her voice: 'Just look at this, it's dead; it's lying here dead and done for!'

Mr and Mrs Samsa started up in their double bed and before they realized the nature of the charwoman's announcement had some difficulty in overcoming the shock of it. But then they got out of bed quickly, one on either side, Mr Samsa throwing a blanket over his shoulders, Mrs Samsa in nothing but her nightgown; in this array they entered Gregor's room. Meanwhile the door of the living-room opened, too, where Grete had been sleeping since the advent of the lodgers; she was completely dressed as if she had not been to bed, which seemed to be confirmed also by the paleness of her face. 'Dead?' said Mrs Samsa, looking questioningly at the charwoman, although she could have investigated for herself, and the fact was obvious enough without investigation. 'I should say so,' said the charwoman, proving her words by pushing Gregor's corpse a long way to one side with her broomstick. Mrs Samsa made a movement as if to stop her, but checked it. 'Well,' said Mr Samsa, 'now thanks be to God.' He crossed himself, and the three women followed his example. Grete, whose eyes never left the corpse, said: 'Just see how thin he was. It's such a long time since he's eaten anything. The food came out again just as it went in.' Indeed, Gregor's body was completely flat and dry, as could only now be seen when it was no longer supported by the legs and nothing prevented one from looking closely at it.

'Come in beside us, Grete, for a little while,' said Mrs Samsa with a tremulous smile, and Grete, not without looking back at the corpse, followed her parents into their bedroom. The charwoman shut the door and opened the window wide. Although it was so early in the morning a certain softness was perceptible in the fresh air. After all, it was already the end of March.

The three lodgers emerged from their room and were surprised to see no breakfast; they had been forgotten. 'Where's our breakfast?' said the middle lodger peevishly to the charwoman. But she put her finger to her lips and hastily, without a word, indicated by gestures that they should go into Gregor's room. They did so and stood, their hands in the pockets of their somewhat shabby coats, around Gregor's corpse in the room where it was now fully light.

At that the door of the Samsas' bedroom opened and Mr Samsa appeared in his uniform, his wife on one arm, his daughter on the other. They all looked a little as if they had been crying; from time to time Grete hid her face on her father's arm.

'Leave my house at once!' said Mr Samsa, and pointed to the door without disengaging himself from the women. 'What do you mean by that?' said the middle lodger, taken somewhat aback, with a feeble smile. The two others put their hands behind them and kept rubbing them together, as if in gleeful expectation of a fine set-to in which they were bound to come off the winners. 'I mean just what I say,' answered Mr Samsa and advanced in a straight line with his two companions towards the lodger. He stood his ground at first quietly, looking at the floor as if his thoughts were taking a new pattern in his head. 'Then let us go, by all means,' he said, and looked up at Mr Samsa as if in a sudden access of humility he were expecting some renewed sanction for this decision. Mr Samsa merely nodded briefly once or twice with meaning eyes. Upon that the lodger really did go with long strides into the hall, his two friends had been listening and had quite stopped rubbing their hands for some moments and now went scuttling after him as if afraid that Mr Samsa might get into the hall before them and cut them off from their leader. In the hall they all three took their hats from the rack, their sticks from the umbrella stand, bowed in silence and quitted the apartment. With a suspiciousness which proved quite unfounded Mr Samsa and the two women followed them out to the landing; leaning over the banisters they watched the three figures slowly but surely going down the long stairs, vanishing from sight at a certain turn of the staircase on every floor and coming into view again after a moment or so; the more they dwindled, the more the Samsa family's interest in them dwindled, and when a butcher's boy met them and passed them on the stairs coming up proudly with a tray on his head, Mr Samsa and the two women soon left the landing and as if a burden had been lifted from them went back into their apartment.

They decided to spend this day in resting and going for a stroll; they had not only deserved such a respite from work, but absolutely needed it. And so they sat down at the table and wrote three notes of excuse; Mr Samsa to his board of management, Mrs Samsa to her employer and Grete to the head of her firm. While they were writing, the charwoman came in to say that she was going now, since her morning's work was finished. At first they only nodded without looking up, but as she kept hovering there they eyed her irritably. 'Well?' said Mr Samsa. The charwoman stood grinning in the doorway as if she had good news to impart to the family but meant not to say a word unless properly questioned. The small ostrich feather standing upright on her hat, which had annoyed Mr Samsa ever since she was engaged, was waving gaily in all directions. 'Well, what is it then?' asked Mrs Samsa, who obtained more respect from the charwoman than the others. 'Oh,' said the charwoman, giggling so amiably that she could not at once continue, 'just this, you don't need to bother about how to get rid of the thing next door. It's been seen to already.' Mrs Samsa and Grete bent over their letters again, as if preoccupied; Mr Samsa, who perceived that she was eager to begin describing it all in detail, stopped her with a decisive hand. But since she was not allowed to tell her story, she remembered the great hurry she was in, being obviously deeply huffed: 'Bye, everybody,' she said, whirling off violently, and departed with a frightful slamming of doors.

'She'll be given notice tonight,' said Mr Samsa, but neither from his wife nor his daughter did he get any answer, for the charwoman seemed to have shattered again the composure they had barely achieved. They rose, went to the window and stayed there, clasping each other tight. Mr Samsa turned in his chair to look at them and quietly observed them for a little. Then he called out: 'Come along, now, do. Let bygones be bygones. And you might have some consideration for me.' The two of them complied at once, hastened to him, caressed him and quickly finished their letters.

Then they all three left the apartment together, which was more than they had done for months, and went by tram into the open country outside the town. The tram, in which they were the only passengers, was filled with warm sunshine. Leaning comfortably back in their seats they canvassed their prospects for the future, and it appeared on closer inspection that these were not at all bad, for the jobs they had got, which so far they had never really discussed with each other, were all three admirable and likely to lead to better things later on. The greatest immediate improvement in their condition would of course arise from moving to another house; they wanted to take a smaller and cheaper but also better situated and more easily run apartment than the one they had, which Gregor had selected. While they were thus conversing, it struck both Mr and Mrs Samsa, almost at the same moment, as they became aware of their daughter's increasing vivacity, that in spite of all the sorrow of recent times, which had made her cheeks pale, she had bloomed into a pretty girl with a good figure. They grew quieter and half unconsciously exchanged glances of complete agreement, having come to the conclusion that it would soon be time to find a good husband for her. And it was like a confirmation of their new dreams and excellent intentions that at the end of their journey their daughter sprang to her feet first and stretched her young body.

The Great Wall of China

THE Great Wall of China was finished off at its northernmost corner. From the south-east and the south-west it came up in two sections that finally converged there. This principle of piecemeal construction was also applied on a smaller scale by both of the two great armies of labour, the eastern and the western. It was done in this way: gangs of some twenty workers were formed who had to accomplish a length, say, of five hundred yards of wall, while a similar gang built another stretch of the same length to meet the first. But after the junction had been made the construction of the wall was not carried on from the point, let us say, where this thousand yards ended; instead the two groups of workers were transferred to begin building again in quite different neighbourhoods. Naturally in this way many great gaps were left, which were only filled in gradually and bit by bit, some, indeed, not till after the official announcement that the wall was finished. In fact it is said that there are gaps which have never been filled in at all, an assertion, however, which is probably merely one of the many legends to which the building of the wall gave rise, and which cannot be verified, at least by any single man with his own eyes and judgement, on account of the extent of the structure.

Now on first thoughts one might conceive that it would have been more advantageous in every way to build the wall continuously, or at least continuously within the two main divisions. After all the wall was intended, as was universally proclaimed and known, to be a protection against the peoples of the north. But how can a wall protect if it is not a continuous structure? Not only cannot such a wall protect, but what there is of it is in perpetual danger. These blocks of wall left standing in deserted regions could be easily pulled down again and again by the nomads, especially as these tribes, rendered apprehensive by the building operations, kept changing their encampments with incredible rapidity, like locusts, and so perhaps had a better general view of the progress of the wall than we, the builders. Nevertheless the task of construction probably could not have been carried out in any other way. To understand this we must take into account the following: The wall was to be a protection for centuries: accordingly the most scrupulous care in the building, the application of the architectural wisdom of all known ages and peoples, an unremitting sense of personal responsibility in the builders, were indispensable prerequisites for the work. True, for the more purely manual tasks ignorant day-labourers from the populace, men, women, and children who offered their services for good money, could be employed; but for the supervision even of four day-labourers an expert versed in the art of building was required, a man who was capable of entering into and feeling with all his heart what was involved. And the higher the task, the greater the responsibility. And such men were actually to be had, if not indeed so abundantly as the work of construction could have absorbed, yet in great numbers.

For the work had not been undertaken without thought. Fifty years before the first stone was laid the art of architecture, and especially that of masonry, had been proclaimed as the most important branch of knowledge throughout the whole area of China that was to be walled round, and all other arts gained recognition only in so far as they had reference to it. I can still remember quite well us standing as small children, scarcely sure on our feet, in our teacher's garden, and being ordered to build a sort of wall out of pebbles; and then the teacher, girding up his robe, ran full tilt against the wall, of course knocking it down, and scolded us so terribly for the shoddiness of our work that we ran weeping in all directions to our parents. A trivial incident, but significant of the spirit of the time.

I was lucky inasmuch as the building of the wall was just beginning when, at twenty, I had passed the last examination of the lowest-grade school. I say lucky, for many who before my time had achieved the highest degree of culture available to them could find nothing year after year to do with their knowledge, and drifted uselessly about with the most splendid architectural plans in their heads, and sank by thousands into hopelessness. But those who finally came to be employed in the work as supervisors, even though it might be of the lowest rank, were truly worthy of their task. They were masons who had reflected much, and did not cease to reflect, on the building of the wall, men who with the first stone which they sank in the ground felt themselves a part of the wall. Masons of that kind, of course, had not only a desire to perform their work in the most thorough manner, but were also impatient to see the wall finished in its complete perfection. Day-labourers have not this impatience, for they look only to their wages, and the higher supervisors, indeed even the supervisors of middle rank, could see enough of the manifold growth of the construction to keep their spirits confident and high. But to encourage the subordinate supervisors, intellectually so vastly superior to their apparently petty tasks, other measures must be taken. One could not, for instance, expect them to lay one stone on another for months or even years on end, in an uninhabited mountainous region, hundreds of miles from their homes; the hopelessness of such hard toil which yet could not reach completion even in the longest lifetime, would have cast them into despair and above all made them less capable for the work. It was for this reason that the system of piecemeal building was decided on. Five hundred yards could be accomplished in about five years; by that time, however, the supervisors were as a rule quite exhausted and had lost all faith in themselves, in the wall, in the world. Accordingly, while they were still exalted by the jubilant celebrations marking the completion of the thousand yards of wall, they were sent far, far away, saw on their journey finished sections of the wall rising here and there, came past the quarters of the high command and were presented with badges of honour, heard the rejoicings of new armies of labour streaming past from the depths of the land, saw forests being cut down to become supports for the wall, saw mountains being hewn into stones for the wall, heard at the holy shrines hymns rising in which the pious prayed for the completion of the wall. All this assuaged their impatience. The quiet life of their homes, where they rested some time, strengthened them; the humble credulity with which their reports were listened to, the confidence with which the simple and peaceful burgher believed in the eventual completion of the wall, all this tightened up again the cords of the soul. Like eternally hopeful children they then said farewell to their homes; the desire once more to labour on the wall of the nation became irresistible. They set off earlier than they needed; half the village accompanied them for long distances. Groups of people with banners and scarfs waving were on all the roads; never before had they seen how great and rich and beautiful and worthy of love their country was. Every fellow-countryman was a brother for whom one was building a wall of protection, and who would return lifelong thanks for it with all he had and did. Unity! Unity! Shoulder to shoulder, a ring of brothers, a current of blood no longer confined within the narrow circulation of one body, but sweetly rolling and yet ever returning throughout the endless leagues of China.

Thus, then, the system of piecemeal construction becomes comprehensible; but there were still other reasons for it as well. Nor is there anything odd in my pausing over this question for so long; it is one of the crucial problems in the whole building of the wall, unimportant as it may appear at first glance. If I am to convey and make understandable the ideas and feelings of that time I cannot go deeply enough into this very question.

First, then, it must be said that in those days things were achieved scarcely inferior to the construction of the Tower of Babel, although as regards divine approval, at least according to human reckoning, strongly at variance with that work. I say this because during the early days of building a scholar wrote a book in which he drew the comparison in the most exhaustive way. In it he tried to prove that the Tower of Babel failed to reach its goal, not because of the reasons universally advanced, or at least that among those recognized reasons the most important of all was not to be found. His proofs were drawn not merely from written documents and reports; he also claimed to have made inquiries on the spot, and to have discovered that the tower failed and was bound to fail because of the weakness of the foundation. In this respect at any rate our age was vastly superior to that ancient one. Almost every educated man of our time was a mason by profession and infallible in the matter of laying foundations. That, however, was not what our scholar was concerned to prove; for he maintained that the Great Wall alone would provide for the first time in the history of mankind a secure foundation for a new Tower of Babel. First the wall, therefore, and then the tower. His book was in everybody's hands at that time, but I admit that even today I cannot quite make out how he conceived this tower. How could the wall, which did not form even a circle, but only a sort of quarter or half-circle, provide the foundation for a tower? That could obviously be meant only in a spiritual sense. But in that case why build the actual wall, which after all was something concrete, the result of the lifelong labour of multitudes of people? And why were there in the book plans, somewhat nebulous plans, it must be admitted, of the tower, and proposals worked out in detail for mobilizing the people's energies for the stupendous new work?

There were many wild ideas in people's heads at that time – this scholar's book is only one example – perhaps simply because so many were trying to join forces as far as they could for the achievement of a single aim. Human nature, essentially changeable, unstable as the dust, can endure no restraint; if it binds itself it soon begins to tear madly at its bonds, until it rends everything asunder, the wall, the bonds and its very self.

It is possible that these very considerations, which militated against the building of the wall at all, were not left out of account by the high command when the system of piecemeal construction was decided on. We – and here I speak in the name of many people – did not really know them ourselves until we had carefully scrutinized the decrees of the high command, when we discovered that without the high command neither our book learning nor our human understanding would have sufficed for the humble tasks which we performed in the great whole. In the office of the command – where it was and who sat there no one whom I have asked knew then or knows now – in that office one may be certain that all human thoughts and desires were revolved, and counter to them all human aims and fulfilments. And through the window the reflected splendours of divine worlds fell on the hands of the leaders as they traced their plans.

And for that reason the incorruptible observer must hold that the command, if it had seriously desired it, could also have overcome those difficulties which prevented a system of continuous construction. There remains, therefore, nothing but the conclusion that the command deliberately chose the system of piecemeal construction. But the piecemeal construction was only a makeshift and therefore inexpedient. Remains the conclusion that the command willed something inexpedient. – Strange conclusion! – True, and yet in one respect it has much to be said for it. One can perhaps safely discuss it now. In those days many people, and among them the best, had a secret maxim which ran: Try with all your might to comprehend the decrees of the high command, but only up to a certain point; then avoid further meditation. A very wise maxim, which moreover was elaborated in a parable that was later often quoted: Avoid further meditation, but not because it might be harmful; it is not at all certain that it would be harmful. What is harmful or not harmful has nothing to do with the question. Consider rather the river in spring. It rises until it grows mightier and nourishes more richly the soil on the long stretch of its banks, still maintaining its own course until it reaches the sea, where it is all the more welcome because it is a worthier ally. – Thus far may you urge your meditations on the decrees of the high command. – But after that the river overflows its banks, loses outline and shape, slows down the speed of its current, tries to ignore its destiny by forming little seas in the interior of the land, damages the fields, and yet cannot maintain itself for long in its new expanse, but must run back between its banks again, must even dry up wretchedly in the hot season that presently follows. – Thus far may you not urge your meditations on the decrees of the high command.

Now though this parable may have had extraordinary point and force during the building of the wall, it has at most only a restricted relevance for my present essay. My inquiry is purely historical; no lightning flashes any longer from the long since vanished thunder-clouds, and so I may venture to seek for an explanation of the system of piecemeal construction which goes farther than the one that contented people then. The limits which my capacity for thought imposes upon me are narrow enough, but the province to be traversed here is infinite. Against whom was the Great Wall to serve as a protection? Against the people of the north. Now, I come from the south-east of China. No northern people can menace us there. We read of them in the books of the ancients; the cruelties which they commit in accordance with their nature make us sigh beneath our peaceful trees. The faithful representations of the artist show us these faces of the damned, their gaping mouths, their jaws furnished with great pointed teeth, their half-shut eyes that already seem to be seeking out the victim whom their jaws will rend and devour. When our children are unruly we show them these pictures, and at once they fly weeping into our arms. But nothing more than that do we know about these northerners. We have not seen them, and if we remain in our villages we shall never see them, even if on their wild horses they should ride as hard as they can straight towards us – the land is too vast and would not let them reach us, they would end their course in the empty air.

Why, then, since that is so, did we leave our homes, the stream with its bridges, our mothers and fathers, our weeping wives, our children who needed our care, and depart for the distant city to be trained there, while our thoughts journeyed still farther away to the wall in the north? Why? A question for the high command. Our leaders know us. They, absorbed in gigantic anxieties, know of us, know our petty pursuits, see us sitting together in our humble huts, and approve or disapprove the evening prayer which the father of the house recites in the midst of his family. And if I may be allowed to express such ideas about the high command, then I must say that in my opinion the high command has existed from old time, and was not assembled, say, like a gathering of mandarins summoned hastily to discuss somebody's fine dream in a conference as hastily terminated, so that that very evening the people are drummed out of their beds to carry out what has been decided, even if it should be nothing but an illumination in honour of a god who may have shown great favour to their masters the day before, only to drive them into some dark corner with cudgel blows tomorrow, almost before the illuminations have died down. Far rather do I believe that the high command has existed from all eternity, and the decision to build the wall likewise. Unwitting peoples of the north, who imagined they were the cause of it! Honest, unwitting Emperor, who imagined he decreed it! We builders of the wall know that it was not so and hold our tongues.

*

During the building of the wall and ever since to this very day I have occupied myself almost exclusively with the comparative history of races – there are certain questions which one can probe to the marrow, as it were, only by this method – and I have discovered that we Chinese possess certain folk and political institutions that are unique in their clarity, others again unique in their obscurity. The desire to trace the causes of these phenomena, especially the latter, has always teased me and teases me still, and the building of the wall is itself essentially involved with these problems.

Now one of the most obscure of our institutions is that of the empire itself. In Pekin, naturally, at the imperial court, there is some clarity to be found on this subject, though even that is more illusive than real. Also the teachers of political law and history in the high schools claim to be exactly informed on these matters, and to be capable of passing on their knowledge to their students. The farther one descends among the lower schools the more, naturally enough, does one find teachers' and pupils' doubts of their own knowledge vanishing, and a superficial culture mounting sky high round a few precepts that have been drilled into people's minds for centuries, precepts which, though they have lost nothing of their eternal truth, remain eternally invisible in this fog of confusion.

But it is precisely this question of the empire which in my opinion the common people should be asked to answer, since after all they are the empire's final support. Here, I must confess, I can only speak once more for my native place. Except for the nature gods and their ritual, which fills the whole year in such beautiful and rich alternation, we think only about the Emperor. But not about the present one; or rather we would think about the present one if we knew who he was or knew anything definite about him. True – and it is the sole curiosity that fills us – we are always trying to get information on this subject, but, strange as it may sound, it is almost impossible to discover anything, either from pilgrims, though they have wandered through many lands, or from near or distant villages, or from sailors, though they have navigated not only our little stream, but also the sacred rivers. One hears a great many things, true, but can gather nothing definite.

So vast is our land that no fable could do justice to its vastness, the heavens can scarcely span it – and Pekin is only a dot in it, and the imperial palace less than a dot. The Emperor as such, on the other hand, is mighty throughout all the hierarchies of the world: admitted. But the existent Emperor, a man like us, lies much like us on a couch which is of generous proportions, perhaps, and yet very possibly may be quite narrow and short. Like us he sometimes stretches himself and when he is very tired yawns with his delicately cut mouth. But how should we know anything about that – thousands of miles away in the south – almost on the borders of the Tibetan Highlands? And besides, any tidings, even if they did reach us, would arrive far too late, would have become obsolete long before they reached us. The Emperor is always surrounded by a brilliant and yet ambiguous throng of nobles and courtiers – malice and enmity in the guise of servants and friends – who form a counter-weight to the Imperial power and perpetually labour to unseat the ruler from his place with poisoned arrows. The Empire is immortal, but the Emperor himself totters and falls from his throne, yes, whole dynasties sink in the end and breathe their last in one death-rattle. Of these struggles and sufferings the people will never know; like tardy arrivals, like strangers in a city, they stand at the end of some densely thronged side street peacefully munching the food they have brought with them, while far away in front, in the market square at the heart of the city, the execution of their ruler is proceeding.

There is a parable which describes this situation very well: The Emperor, so it runs, has sent a message to you, the humble subject, the insignificant shadow cowering in the remotest distance before the imperial sun; the Emperor from his death-bed has sent a message to you alone. He has commanded the messenger to kneel down by the bed, and has whispered the message to him; so much store did he lay on it that he ordered the messenger to whisper it back into his ear again. Then by a nod of the head he has confirmed that it is right. Yes, before the assembled spectators of his death – all the obstructing walls have been broken down, and on the spacious and loftily mounting open staircases stand in a ring the great princes of the Empire – before all these he has delivered his message. The messenger immediately sets out on his journey; a powerful, an indefatigable man; now pushing with his right arm, now with his left, he cleaves a way for himself through the throng; if he encounters resistance he points to his breast, where the symbol of the sun glitters; the way, too, is made easier for him than it would be for any other man. But the multitudes are so vast; their numbers have no end. If he could reach the open fields how fast he would fly, and soon doubtless you would hear the welcome hammering of his fists on your door. But instead how vainly does he wear out his strength; still he is only making his way through the chambers of the innermost palace; never will he get to the end of them; and if he succeeded in that nothing would be gained; he must fight his way next down the stairs; and if he succeeded in that nothing would be gained; the courts would still have to be crossed; and after the courts the second outer palace; and once more stairs and courts; and once more another palace; and so on for thousands of years; and if at last he should burst through the outermost gate – but never, never can that happen – the imperial capital would lie before him, the centre of the world, crammed to bursting with its own refuse. Nobody could fight his way through here even with a message from a dead man. – But you sit at your window when evening falls and dream it to yourself.

Just so, as hopelessly and as hopefully, do our people regard the Emperor. They do not know what emperor is reigning, and there exist doubts regarding even the name of the dynasty. In school a great deal is taught about the dynasties with the dates of succession, but the universal uncertainty on this matter is so great that even the best scholars are drawn into it. Long-dead emperors are set on the throne in our villages, and one that only lives in song recently had a proclamation of his read out by the priest before the altar. Battles that are old history are new to us, and one's neighbour rushes in with a jubilant face to tell the news. The wives of the emperors, pampered and overweening, seduced from noble custom by wily courtiers, swelling with ambition, vehement in their greed, uncontrollable in their lust, practise their abominations ever anew. The more deeply they are buried in time the more glaring are the colours in which their deeds are painted, and with a loud cry of woe our village eventually hears how an Empress drank her husband's blood in long draughts thousands of years ago.

Thus, then, do our people deal with departed emperors, but the living ruler they confuse among the dead. If once, only once in a man's lifetime, an imperial official on his tour of the provinces should arrive by chance at our village, make certain announcements in the name of the government, scrutinize the tax lists, examine the school children, inquire of the priest regarding our doings and affairs, and then, before he steps into his litter, should sum up his impressions in verbose admonitions to the assembled commune – then a smile flits over every face, each man throws a stolen glance at his neighbour, and bends over his children so as not to be observed by the official. Why, they think to themselves, he's speaking of a dead man as if he were alive, this Emperor of his died long ago, the dynasty is blotted out, the good official is having his joke with us, but we will behave as if we did not notice it, so as not to offend him. But we shall obey in earnest no one but our present ruler, for to do so would be a crime. And behind the departing litter of the official there arises in might as ruler of the village some figure fortuitously exalted from an urn already crumbled to dust.

Similarly our people are but little affected by revolutions in the state or contemporary wars. I recall an incident in my youth. A revolt had broken out in a neighbouring, but yet quite distant, province. What caused it I can no longer remember, nor is it of any importance now; occasions for revolt can be found there any day, the people are an excitable people. Well, one day a leaflet published by the rebels was brought to my father's house by a beggar who had crossed that province. It happened to be a feast day, our rooms were filled with guests, the priest sat in the chief place and studied the sheet. Suddenly everybody started to laugh, in the confusion the sheet was torn, the beggar, who however had already received abundant alms, was driven out of the room with blows, the guests dispersed to enjoy the beautiful day. Why? The dialect of this neighbouring province differs in some essential respects from ours, and this difference occurs also in certain turns of the written speech, which for us have an archaic character. Hardly had the priest read out two lines before we had already come to our decision. Ancient history told long ago, old sorrows long since healed. And though – so it seems to me in recollection – the gruesomeness of the living present was irrefutably conveyed by the beggar's words, we laughed and shook our heads and refused to listen any longer. So eager are our people to obliterate the present.

If from such appearances any one should draw the conclusion that in reality we have no Emperor, he would not be far from the truth. Over and over again it must be repeated: There is perhaps no people more faithful to the Emperor than ours in the south, but the Emperor derives no advantage from our fidelity. True, the sacred dragon stands on the little column at the end of our village, and ever since the beginning of human memory it has breathed out its fiery breath in the direction of Pekin in token of homage – but Pekin itself is far stranger to the people in our village than the next world. Can there really be a village where the houses stand side by side, covering all the fields for a greater distance than one can see from our hills, and can there be dense crowds of people packed between these houses day and night? We find it more difficult to picture such a city than to believe that Pekin and its Emperor are one, a cloud, say, peacefully voyaging beneath the sun in the course of the ages.

Now the result of holding such opinions is a life on the whole free and unconstrained. By no means immoral, however; hardly ever have I found in my travels such pure morals as in my native village. But yet a life that is subject to no contemporary law, and attends only to the exhortations and warnings which come to us from olden times.

I guard against large generalizations, and do not assert that in all the countless villages in my province it is so, far less in all the five hundred provinces of China. Yet perhaps I may venture to assert on the basis of the many writings on this subject which I have read, as well as from my own observation – the building of the wall in particular, with its abundance of human material, provided a man of sensibility with the opportunity of traversing the souls of almost all the provinces – on the basis of all this, then, perhaps I may venture to assert that the prevailing attitude to the Emperor shows persistently and universally something fundamentally in common with that of our village. Now I have no wish whatever to represent this attitude as a virtue; on the contrary. True, the essential responsibility for it lies with the government, which in the most ancient empire in the world has not yet succeeded in developing, or has neglected to develop, the institution of the empire to such precision that its workings extend directly and unceasingly to the farthest frontiers of the land. On the other hand, however, there is also involved a certain feebleness of faith and imaginative power on the part of the people, that prevents them from raising the empire out of its stagnation in Pekin and clasping it in all its palpable living reality to their own breasts, which yet desire nothing better than but once to feel that touch and then to die.

This attitude then is certainly no virtue. All the more remarkable is it that this very weakness should seem to be one of the greatest unifying influences among our people; indeed, if one may dare to use the expression, the very ground on which we live. To set about establishing a fundamental defect here would mean undermining not only our consciences, but, what is far worse, our feet. And for that reason I shall not proceed any further at this stage with my inquiry into these questions.

Investigations of a Dog

How much my life has changed, and yet how unchanged it has remained at bottom! When I think back and recall the time when I was still a member of the canine community, sharing in all its preoccupations, a dog among dogs, I find on closer examination that from the very beginning I sensed some discrepancy, some little maladjustment, causing a slight feeling of discomfort which not even the most decorous public functions could eliminate; more, that sometimes, no, not sometimes, but very often, the mere look of some fellow-dog of my own circle that I was fond of, the mere look of him, as if I had just caught it for the first time, would fill me with helpless embarrassment and fear, even with despair. I tried to quiet my apprehensions as best I could; friends, to whom I divulged them, helped me; more peaceful times came – times, it is true, in which these sudden surprises were not lacking, but in which they were accepted with more philosophy, fitted into my life with more philosophy, inducing a certain melancholy and lethargy, it may be, but nevertheless allowing me to carry on as a somewhat cold, reserved, shy and calculating, but, all things considered, normal enough dog. How, indeed, without these intervals of convalescence, could I have reached the age that I enjoy at present; how could I have fought my way through to the serenity with which I contemplate the terrors of youth and endure the terrors of age; how could I have come to the point where I am able to draw the consequences of my admittedly unhappy, or, to put it more moderately, not very happy position, and live almost entirely in accordance with them? Solitary and withdrawn, with nothing to occupy me save my hopeless but, as far as I am concerned, indispensable little investigations, that is how I live; yet in my distant isolation I have not lost sight of my people, news often penetrates to me, and now and then I even let news of myself reach them. The others treat me with respect but do not understand my way of life; yet they bear me no grudge, and even young dogs whom I sometimes see passing in the distance, a new generation of whose childhood I have only a vague memory, do not deny me a reverential greeting.

For it must not be assumed that, for all my peculiarities, which lie open to the day, I am in the least exempt from the laws of my species. Indeed when I reflect on it – and I have time and disposition and capacity enough for that – I see that dogdom is in every way a marvellous institution. Apart from us dogs there are all sorts of creatures in the world, wretched, limited, dumb creatures who have no language but mechanical cries: many of us dogs study them, having given them names, try to help them, educate them, uplift them, and so on. For my part I am quite indifferent to them except when they try to disturb me, I confuse them with one another, I ignore them. But one thing is too obvious to have escaped me; namely, how little inclined they are, compared with us dogs, to stick together, how silently and unfamiliarly and with what a curious hostility they pass each other by, how mean are the interests that suffice to bind them together for a little in ostensible union, and how often these very interests give rise to hatred and conflict. Consider us dogs, on the other hand! One can safely say that we all live together in a literal heap, all of us, different as we are from one another on account of numberless and profound modifications which have arisen in the course of time. All in one heap! We are drawn to each other and nothing can prevent us from satisfying that communal impulse; all our laws and institutions, the few that I still know and the many that I have forgotten, go back to this longing for the greatest bliss we are capable of, the warm comfort of being together. But now consider the other side of the picture. No creatures to my knowledge live in such wide dispersion as we dogs, none have so many distinctions of class, of kind, of occupation, distinctions too numerous to review at a glance; we, whose one desire is to stick together – and again and again we succeed at transcendent moments in spite of everything – we above all others are compelled to live separated from one another by strange vocations that are often incomprehensible even to our canine neighbours, holding firmly to laws that are not those of the dog world, but are actually directed against it. How baffling these questions are, questions on which one would prefer not to touch – I understand that standpoint too, even better than my own – and yet questions to which I have completely capitulated. Why do I not do as the others: live in harmony with my people and accept in silence whatever disturbs the harmony, ignoring it as a small error in the great account, always keeping in mind the things that bind us happily together, not those that drive us again and again, although by sheer force, out of our social circle?

I can recall an incident in my youth; I was at the time in one of those inexplicable blissful states of exaltation which every one must have experienced as a child; I was still quite a puppy, everything pleased me, everything was my concern, I believed that great things were going on around me of which I was the leader and to which I must lend my voice, things which must be wretchedly thrown aside if I did not run for them and wag my tail for them – childish fantasies that fled with riper years. But at the time their power was very great, I was completely under their spell, and presently something actually did happen, something so extraordinary that it seemed to justify my wild expectations. In itself it was nothing very extraordinary, for I have seen many such things, and more remarkable things too, often enough since, but at the time it struck me with all the force of a first impression, one of those impressions which can never be erased and influence much of one's later conduct. I encountered, in short, a little company of dogs, or rather I did not encounter them, they appeared before me. Before that I had been running along in darkness for some time, filled with a premonition of great things – a premonition that may well have been delusive,

for I always had it. I had run in darkness for a long time, up
and down, blind and deaf to everything, led on by nothing but
a vague desire, and now I suddenly came to a stop with the
feeling that I was in the right place, and looking up saw that it
was bright day, only a little hazy, and everywhere a blending
and confusion of the most intoxicating smells; I greeted the
morning with an uncertain barking, when – as if I had con-
jured them up – out of some place of darkness, to the accom-
paniment of terrible sounds such as I had never heard before,
seven dogs stepped into the light. Had I not distinctly seen that
they were dogs and that they themselves brought the sound
with them – though I could not recognize how they produced
it – I would have run away at once; but as it was I stayed. At
that time I still knew hardly anything of the creative gift for
music with which the canine race alone is endowed, it had
naturally enough escaped my but slowly developing powers of
observation; for though music had surrounded me as a perfectly natural and indispensable element of existence ever since
I was a suckling, an element which nothing impelled me to
distinguish from the rest of existence, my elders had drawn my
attention to it only by such hints as were suitable for a childish
understanding; all the more astonishing, then, indeed devast-
ating, were these seven great musical artists to me. They did
not speak, they did not sing, they remained, all of them, silent,
almost determinedly silent; but from the empty air they con-
jured music. Everything was music, the lifting and setting down
of their feet, certain turns of the head, their running and their
standing still, the positions they took up in relation to one
another, the symmetrical patterns which they produced by one
dog setting his front paws on the back of another and the rest
following suit until the first bore the weight of the other six, or
lying flat on the ground and then crawling through complicated
concerted evolutions; and none made a false move, not even
the last dog, though he was a little unsure, did not always
establish contact at once with the others, sometimes hesitated,

as it were, on the stroke of the beat, but yet was unsure only by comparison with the superb sureness of the others, and even if he had been much more unsure, indeed quite unsure, would not have been able to do any harm, the others, great masters all of them keeping the rhythm so unshakably. But it is too much to say that I saw them clearly, that I actually even saw them. They appeared from somewhere, I inwardly greeted them as dogs, and although I was profoundly confused by the sounds that accompanied them, yet they were dogs nevertheless, dogs like you and me; I regarded them by force of habit simply as dogs I had happened to meet on my road, and felt a wish to approach them and exchange greetings; they were quite near too, dogs much older than me, certainly, and not of my woolly, long-haired kind, but yet not so very alien in size and shape, indeed quite familiar to me, for I had already seen many such or similar dogs; but while I was still involved in these reflections the music insensibly got the upper hand, literally knocked the breath out of me and swept me far away from those actual little dogs, and quite against my will, while I howled as if some pain were being inflicted upon me, my mind could attend to nothing but this blast of music which seemed to come from all sides, from the heights, from the deeps, from everywhere, seizing the listener by the middle, overwhelming him, crushing him, and over his swooning body still blowing fanfares so near that they seemed far away and almost inaudible. And then a respite came, for one was already too exhausted, too annulled, too feeble to listen any longer; a respite came and I beheld again the seven little dogs carrying out their evolutions, making their leaps; I longed to shout to them in spite of their aloofness, to beg them to enlighten me, to ask them what they were doing – I was a child and believed I could ask anybody about anything – but hardly had I begun, hardly did I feel on good and familiar dog-gish terms with the seven, when the music started again, robbed me of my wits, whirled me round in its circles as if I myself were one of the musicians instead of being only their victim, cast me hither and thither, no matter how much I begged for mercy, and rescued me finally from its own violence by driving me into a labyrinth of wooden bars which rose round that place, though I had not noticed it before, but which now firmly caught me, kept my head pressed to the ground, and though the music still resounded in the open space behind me, gave me a little time to get my breath back. I must admit that I was less surprised by the artistry of the seven dogs – it was incomprehensible to me, and also quite definitely beyond my capacities – than by their courage in facing so openly the music of their own making, and their power to endure it calmly without collapsing. But now from my hiding-place I saw, on looking more closely, that it was not so much coolness as the most extreme tension that characterized their performance; these limbs apparently so sure in their movements quivered at every step with a perpetual apprehensive twitching; as if rigid with despair the dogs kept their eyes fixed on one another, and their tongues, whenever the tension weakened for a moment, hung wearily from their jowls. It could not be fear of failure that agitated them so deeply; dogs that could dare and achieve such things had no need to fear that. Then why were they afraid? Who then forced them to do what they were doing? And I could no longer restrain myself, particularly as they now seemed in some incomprehensible way in need of help, and so through all the din of the music I shouted out my questions loudly and challengingly. But they – incredible! incredible! – they never replied, behaved as if I were not there. Dogs who make no reply to the greeting of other dogs are guilty of an offence against good manners which the humblest dog would never pardon any more than the greatest. Perhaps they were not dogs at all? But how should they not be dogs? Could I not actually hear on listening more closely the subdued cries with which they encouraged each other, drew each other's attention to difficulties, warned each other against errors; could I not see the last and youngest dog, to whom most of those cries were addressed,

often stealing a glance at me as if he would have dearly wished
to reply, but refrained because it was not allowed? But why
should it not be allowed, why should the very thing which our
laws unconditionally command not be allowed in this one case?
I became indignant at the thought and almost forgot the music.
Those dogs were violating the law. Great magicians they might
be, but the law was valid for them too; I knew that quite well
though I was a child. And having recognized that I now noticed
something else. They had good grounds for remaining silent,
that is, assuming that they remained silent from a sense of
shame. For how were they conducting themselves? Because of
all the music I had not noticed it before, but they had flung
away all shame, the wretched creatures were doing the very
thing which is both most ridiculous and indecent in our eyes;
they were walking on their hind legs. Fie on them! They were
uncovering their nakedness, blatantly making a show of their
nakedness, they were doing that as though it were a meritori-
ous act, and when, obeying their better instincts for a moment,
they happened to let their front paws fall, they were literally
appalled as if at an error, as if Nature were an error, hastily
raised their legs again, and their eyes seemed to be begging
forgiveness for having been forced to cease momentarily from
their abomination. Was the world standing on its head? Where
could I be? What could have happened? If only for my own sake
I dared not hesitate any longer now, I dislodged myself from
the tangle of bars, took one leap into the open and made towards the dogs – I, the younger scholar, must be the teacher
now, must make them understand what they were doing, must
keep them from committing further sin. 'And old dogs too!
And old dogs too!' I kept on saying to myself. But scarcely was
I free and only a leap or two away from the dogs, when the
music again had me in its power. Perhaps in my ardour I might
even have managed to withstand it, for I knew it better now, if
in the midst of all its majestic amplitude, which was terrifying,
but still not unconquerable, a clear, piercing, continuous note

which came without variation literally from the remotest distance – perhaps the real melody in the midst of the music – had not now rung out, forcing me to my knees. Oh, the music these dogs made almost drove me out of my senses! I could not move a step farther, I no longer wanted to instruct them; they could go on raising their front legs, committing sin and seducing others to the sin of silently regarding them; I was such a young dog – who could demand such a difficult task from me? I made myself still more insignificant than I was, I whimpered, and if the dogs had asked me now what I thought of their performance, probably I would have had not a word to say against it. Besides it was not long before the dogs vanished with all their music and their radiance into the darkness from which they had emerged.

As I have already said, this whole episode contains nothing of much note; in the course of a long life one encounters all sorts of things which, taken from their context and seen through the eyes of a child, might well seem far more astonishing. Besides, one may, of course – in the pungent popular phrase – have 'got it all wrong', as well as everything connected with it; then it could be demonstrated that this was simply a case where seven musicians had assembled to practise their art in the morning stillness, that a very young dog had strayed to the place, a burdensome intruder whom they had tried to drive away by particularly terrifying or lofty music, unfortunately without success. He pestered them with his questions; were they, already disturbed enough by the mere presence of the stranger, to be expected to attend to his distracting interruptions as well and make them worse by responding to them? Even if the law commands us to reply to everybody, was such a tiny stray dog in truth a somebody worth regarding? And perhaps they did not even understand him, for likely enough he barked his questions very indistinctly. Or perhaps they did understand him and with great self-control answered his questions, but he, a mere puppy unaccustomed to music, could not distinguish the answer from the music. And as for walking on their hind legs, perhaps, unlike other dogs, they actually used only these for walking; if it was a sin, well it was a sin. But they were alone, seven friends together, an intimate gathering within their own four walls so to speak, quite private so to speak; for one's friends, after all, are not the public, and where the public is not present an inquisitive little street dog is certainly not capable of constituting it; but, granting this, is it not as if nothing at all had happened? It is not quite so, but very nearly so, and parents should not let their children run about so freely, and had much better teach them to hold their tongues and respect the aged.

If all this is admitted, then it disposes of the whole case. But many things that are disposed of in the minds of grown-ups are not yet settled in the minds of the young. I rushed about, told my story, asked questions, made accusations and investigations, tried to drag others to the place where all this had happened, and burned to show everybody where I had stood and where the seven had stood, and where and how they had danced and made their music; and if any one had come with me, instead of shaking me off and laughing at me, I would probably have sacrificed my innocence and tried myself to stand on my hind legs so as to reconstruct the scene clearly. Now children are blamed for all they do, but also in the last resort forgiven for all they do. And I have preserved my childish qualities, and in spite of that have grown to be an old dog. Well, just as at that time I kept on unceasingly discussing the foregoing incident – which today I must confess I lay far less importance upon – analysing it into its constituent parts, arguing it with my listeners without regard to the company I found myself in, devoting my whole time to the problem, which I found as wearisome as everybody else, but which – that was the difference – for that very reason I was resolved to pursue indefatigably until I solved it, so that I might be left free to regain the ordinary, calm, happy life of every day: just so have I, though with less childish means – yet the difference is not so very great – laboured in the years since and go on labouring today.

But it began with that concert. I do not blame the concert; it is my innate disposition that has driven me on, and it would certainly have found some other opportunity of coming into action had the concert never taken place. Yet the fact that it happened so soon used to make me feel sorry for myself; it robbed me of a great part of my childhood; the blissful life of the young dog, which many can spin out for years, in my case lasted for only a few short months. So be it. There are more important things than childhood. And perhaps I have the prospect of far more childish happiness, earned by a life of hard work, in my old age than any actual child would have the strength to bear, but which then I shall possess.

I began my inquiries with the simplest things; there was no lack of material; it is the actual superabundance, unfortunately, that casts me into despair in my darker hours. I began to inquire into the question: What the canine race nourished itself upon? Now that is, if you like, by no means a simple question, of course; it has occupied us since the dawn of time, it is the chief object of all our meditation, countless observations and essays and views on this subject have been published, it has grown into a province of knowledge which in its prodigious compass is not only beyond the comprehension of any single scholar, but of all our scholars collectively, a burden which cannot be borne except by the whole of the dog community, and even then not without difficulty and only in part; for it ever and again crumbles away like a neglected ancestral inheritance and must laboriously be rehabilitated anew – not to speak at all of the difficulties and almost unfulfillable conditions of my investigation. No one need point all this out to me, I know it all as well as any average sensual dog can do; I have no ambition to meddle with real scientific matters, I have all the respect for knowledge that it deserves, but to increase knowledge I lack the equipment, the diligence, the leisure, and – not least, and particularly during the past few years – the desire as well. I swallow down my food, but the slightest preliminary methodical politico-economical observation of it does not seem to me worth while. In this connexion the essence of all knowledge is enough for me, the simple rule with which the mother weans her young ones from her teats and sends them out into the world: 'Water the ground as much as you can.' And is not almost everything contained in that? What has scientific inquiry, ever since our first fathers inaugurated it, of decisive importance to add to it? Mere details, mere details, and how uncertain they are: but this rule will remain as long as we are dogs. It concerns our staple food: true, we have also other resources, but only at a pinch, and if the year is not too bad we could live on this staple food; we find it in the earth, but the earth needs our water to nourish it and only at that price provides us with our food, the emergence of which, however, and this should not be forgotten, can also be hastened by certain spells, songs, and ritual movements. But in my opinion that is all; there is nothing else that is fundamental to be said on the question. In this opinion, moreover, I am at one with the vast majority of the dog community, and must firmly dissociate myself from all heretical views on this point. Quite honestly I have no ambition to be peculiar, or to pose as being in the right against the majority; I am only too happy when I can agree with my comrades, as I do in this case. My own inquiries, however, are in another direction. My personal observation tells me that the earth, when it is watered and scratched according to the rules of science, extrudes nourishment, and moreover in such quality, in such abundance, in such ways, in such places, at such hours, as the laws partially or completely established by science demand. I accept all this; my question, however, is the following: 'Whence does the earth procure this food?' A question which people in general pretend not to understand, and to which the best answer they can give is: 'If you haven't enough to eat, we'll give you some of ours.' Now consider this answer. I know that it is not one of the virtues of dogdom to share with others food that one has once gained possession of. Life is hard, the earth stubborn, science rich in knowledge but poor in practical results: anyone who has food keeps it to himself; that is not selfishness, but the opposite, dog law, the unanimous decision of the people, the outcome of their victory over egoism, for the possessors are always in a minority. And for that reason this answer: 'If you haven't enough to eat, we'll give you some of ours' is merely a way of speaking, a jest, a form of raillery. I have not forgotten that. But all the more significant did it seem to me, when I was rushing about everywhere with my questions during those days, that they put the jest aside as far as I was concerned; true, they did not actually give me anything to eat – where could they have found it at a moment's notice? – and even if anyone chanced to have some food, naturally he forgot everything else in the fury of his hunger; yet they all seriously meant what they said when they made the offer, and here and there, right enough, I was presently allowed some slight trifle if I was only smart enough to snatch it quickly. How came it that people treated me so strangely, pampered me, favoured me? Because I was a lean dog, badly fed and neglectful of my needs? But there were countless badly fed dogs running about, and the others snatched even the wretchedest scrap from under their noses whenever they could, and not often from greed, but generally on principle. No, they treated me with special favour; I cannot give much detailed proof of this, but I have a firm conviction that it was so. Was it my questions, then, that pleased them, and that they regarded as so clever? No, my questions did not please them and were generally looked on as stupid. And yet it could only have been my questions that won me their attention. It was as if they would rather do the impossible, that is stop my mouth with food – they did not do it, but they would have liked to do it – than endure my questions. But in that case they would have done better to drive me away and refuse to listen to my questions. No, they did not want to do that; they did not indeed want to listen to my questions, but it was because I asked questions that they did not want to drive me away. That was the time – much as I was ridiculed and treated as a silly puppy, and pushed here and pushed there – the time when I actually enjoyed most public esteem; never again was I to enjoy anything like it; I had free entry everywhere, no obstacle was put in my way, I was actually flattered, though the flattery was disguised as rudeness. And all really because of my questions, my impatience, my thirst for knowledge. Did they want to lull me to sleep, to divert me, without violence, almost lovingly, from a path that was false, yet not so completely false that violence was permissible? – also a certain respect and fear kept them from employing violence. I divined even in those days something of this; today I know it quite well, far better than those who actually practised it at the time: what they wanted to do was really to divert me from my path. They did not succeed; they achieved the opposite; my vigilance was sharpened. More, it became clear to me that it was I who was trying to seduce the others, and that I was actually successful up to a certain point. Only with the assistance of the whole dog world could I begin to understand my own questions. For instance when I asked: 'Whence does the earth procure this food?' was I troubled, as appearances might quite well indicate, about the earth; was I troubled about the labours of the earth? Not in the least; that, as I very soon recognized, was far from my mind; all that I cared for was the race of dogs, that and nothing else. For what is there actually except our own species? To whom else can one appeal in the wide and empty world? All knowledge, the totality of all questions and all answers, is contained in the dog. If one could but realize this knowledge, if one could but bring it into the light of day, if we dogs would but own that we know infinitely more than we admit to ourselves! Even the most loquacious dog is more secretive of his knowledge than of the places where good food can be found. Trembling with desire, whipping yourself with your own tail, you steal cautiously upon your fellow-dog, you ask, you beg, you howl, you bite, and achieve – and achieve what you could have achieved just as well without any effort: amiable attention, friendly contiguity, honest acceptance, ardent embraces, barks that mingle as one: everything is directed towards achieving an ecstasy, a forgetting and finding again; but the one thing that you long to win above all, the admission of knowledge, remains denied to you. To such prayers, whether silent or loud, the only answer you get, even after you have employed your powers of seduction to the utmost, are vacant stares, averted glances, troubled and veiled eyes. It is much the same as it was when, a mere puppy, I shouted to the dog musicians and they remained silent.

Now one might say: 'You torment yourself because of your fellow-dogs, because of their silence on crucial questions; you assert that they know more than they admit, more than they will allow to be valid, and that this silence, the mysterious reason for which is also, of course, tacitly concealed, poisons existence and makes it unendurable for you, so that you must either alter it or have done with it; that may be; but you are yourself a dog, you have also the dog knowledge; well, bring it out, not merely in the form of a question, but as an answer. If you utter it, who will think of opposing you? The great choir of dogdom will join in as if it had been waiting for you. Then you will have clarity, truth, avowal, as much of them as you desire. The roof of this wretched life, of which you say so many hard things, will burst open, and all of us, shoulder to shoulder, will ascend into the lofty realm of freedom. And if we should not achieve that final consummation, if things should become worse than before, if the whole truth should be more insupportable than the half, if it should be proved that the silent are in the right as the guardians of existence, if the faint hope that we still possess should give way to complete hopelessness, the attempt is still worth the trial, since you do not desire to live as you are compelled to live. Well, then, why do you make it a reproach against the others that they are silent, and remain silent yourself?' Easy to answer: Because I am a dog; in essentials just as locked in silence as the others, stubbornly resisting my own questions, dour out of fear. To be precise, is it in the hope that they might answer me that I have questioned my fellow-dogs, at least since my adult years? Have I any such foolish hope? Can I contemplate the foundations of our existence, divine their profundity, watch the labour of their construction, that dark labour, and expect all this to be forsaken, neglected, undone, simply because I ask a question? No, that I truly expect no longer. I understand my fellow-dogs, am flesh of their flesh, of their miserable ever-renewed, ever desirous flesh. Yet it is not merely flesh and blood that we have in common, but knowledge also, and not only knowledge, but the key to it as well. I do not possess that key except in common with all the others; I cannot grasp it without their help. The hardest bones, containing the richest marrow, can be conquered only by a united crunching of all the teeth of all dogs. That, of course, is only a figure of speech and exaggerated; if all teeth were but ready they would not need even to bite, the bones would crack themselves and the marrow would be freely accessible to the feeblest of dogs. If I remain faithful to this metaphor, then the goal of my aims, my questions, my inquiries, appears monstrous, it is true. For I want to compel all dogs thus to assemble together, I want the bones to crack open under the pressure of this collective preparedness, and then I want to dismiss them to the ordinary life that they love, while all by myself, quite alone, I lap up the marrow. That sounds monstrous, almost as if I wanted to feed on the marrow, not merely of a bone, but of the whole canine race itself. But it is only a metaphor. The marrow that I am discussing here is no food; on the contrary, it is a poison.

My questions only serve as a goad to myself; I only want to be stimulated by the silence which rises up around me as the ultimate answer. 'How long will you be able to endure the fact that the world of dogs, as your researches make more and more evident, is pledged to silence and always will be? How long will you be able to endure it?' That is the real great question of my life, before which all smaller ones sink into insignificance; it is put to myself alone and concerns no one else. Unfortunately I can answer it more easily than the smaller, specific questions: I shall probably hold out till my natural end; the calm of old age will put up a greater and greater resistance to all disturbing questions. I shall very likely die in silence and surrounded by silence, indeed almost peacefully, and I look forward to that with composure. An admirably strong heart, lungs that it is impossible to use up before their time, have been given to us dogs as if in malice; we survive all questions, even our own, bulwarks of silence that we are.

Recently I have taken more and more to examining my life, looking for the decisive, the fundamental, error that I must surely have made; and I cannot find it. And yet I must have made it, for if I had not made it and yet were unable by the diligent labour of a long life to achieve my desire, that would prove that my desire is impossible, and complete hopelesness must follow. Behold, then, the work of a lifetime. First of all my inquiries into the question: Whence does the earth procure the food it gives us? A young dog, at bottom naturally greedy for life, I renounced all enjoyments, apprehensively avoided all pleasures, buried my head between my front paws when I was confronted by temptation, and addressed myself to my task. I was no scholar, neither in the information I acquired, nor in method, nor in intention. That was probably a defect, but it could not have been a decisive one. I had had little schooling, for I left my mother's care at an early age, soon got used to independence, led a free life; and premature independence is inimical to systematic learning. But I have seen much, listened to much, spoken with dogs of all sorts and conditions, understood everything, I believe, fairly intelligently, and correlated my particular observations fairly intelligently: that has compensated somewhat for my lack of scholarship, not to mention that independence, if it is a disadvantage in learning things, is an actual advantage when one is making one's own inquiries. In my case it was all the more necessary as I was not able to employ the real method of science, to avail myself, that is, of the labours of my predecessors, and establish contact with contemporary investigators. I was entirely cast on my own resources, began at the very beginning, and with the consciousness, inspiriting to youth, but utterly crushing to age, that the fortuitous point to which I carried my labours must also be the final one. Was I really so alone in my inquiries, at the beginning and up to now? Yes and no. It is inconceivable that there must not always have been and that there are not today individual dogs in the same case as myself. I cannot be so accursed as that. I do not deviate from the dog nature by a hairbreadth. Every dog has like me the impulse to question, and I have like every dog the impulse not to answer. Every one has the impulse to question. How otherwise could my questions have affected my hearers in the slightest – and they were often affected, to my ecstatic delight, an exaggerated delight, I must confess – and how otherwise could I have been prevented from achieving much more than I have done? And that I have the compulsion to remain silent needs unfortunately no particular proof. I am at bottom, then, no different from any other dog; everybody, no matter how he may differ in opinion from me and reject my views, will gladly admit that, and I in turn will admit as much of any other dog. Only the mixture of the elements is different, a difference very important for the individual, significant for the race. And how can one credit that the composition of these available elements has never chanced through all the past and present to result in a mixture similar to mine, one, moreover, if mine be regarded as unfortunate, more unfortunate still? To think so would be contrary to all experience. We dogs are all engaged in the strangest occupations, occupations in which one would refuse to believe if one had not the most reliable information concerning them. The best example I can quote is that of the hovering dog. The first time I heard of one I laughed and simply refused to believe it. What? One was asked to believe that there was a very tiny species of dog, not much bigger than my head even when it was full grown, and this dog, who must of course be a feeble creature, an artificial, weedy, brushed and curled fop by all accounts, incapable of making an honest jump, this dog was supposed, according to people's stories, to remain for the most part high up in the air, apparently doing nothing at all but simply resting there? No, to try to make me swallow such things was exploiting the simplicity of a young dog too outrageously, I told myself. But shortly afterwards I heard from another source an account of another hovering dog. Could there be a conspiracy to fool me? But after that I saw the dog musicians with my own eyes, and from that day I considered everything possible, no prejudices fettered my powers of apprehension, I investigated the most senseless rumours, following them as far as they could take me, and the most senseless seemed to me in this senseless world more probable than the sensible, and moreover particularly fertile for investigation. So it was too with the hovering dogs. I discovered a great many things about them; true, I have succeeded to this day in seeing none of them, but of their existence I have been firmly convinced for a long time, and they occupy an important place in my picture of the world. As usual it is not, of course, their technique that chiefly gives me to think. It is wonderful – who can gainsay it? – that these dogs should be able to float in the air: in my amazed admiration for that I am at one with my fellow-dogs. But far more strange to my mind is the senselessness, the senselessness of these existences. They have no relation whatever to the general life of the community, they hover in the air, and that is all, and life goes on its usual way; someone now and then refers to art and artists, but there it ends. But why, my good dogs, why on earth do these dogs float in the air? What sense is there in their occupation? Why can one get no word of explanation regarding them? Why do they hover up there, letting their legs, the pride of dogs, fall into desuetude, preserving a detachment from the nourishing earth, reaping without having sowed? being particularly well provided for as I hear, and at the cost of the dog community too. I can flatter myself that my inquiries into these matters made some stir. People began to investigate after a fashion, to collect data; they made a beginning, at least, although they are never likely to go farther. But after all that is something. And though the truth will not be discovered by such means – never can that stage be reached – yet they throw light on some of the profounder ramifications of falsehood. For all the senseless phenomena of our existence, and the most senseless most of all, are susceptible of investigation. Not completely, of course – that is the diabolical jest – but sufficiently to spare one painful questions. Take the hovering dogs once more as an example; they are not haughty as one might imagine at first, but rather particularly dependent upon their fellow-dogs; if one tries to put oneself in their place one will see that. For they must do what they can to obtain pardon, and not openly – that would be a violation of the obligation to keep silence – they must do what they can to obtain pardon for their way of life, or else divert attention from it so that it may be forgotten – and they do this, I have been told, by means of an almost unendurable volubility. They are perpetually talking, partly of their philosophical reflections, with which, seeing that they have completely renounced bodily exertion, they can continuously occupy themselves, partly of the observations which they have made from their exalted stations; and although, as is very understandable considering their lazy existence, they are not much distinguished for intellectual power, and their philosophy is as worthless as their observations, and science can make hardly any use of their utterances, and besides is not reduced to draw assistance from such wretched sources, nevertheless if one asks what the hovering dogs are really doing one will invariably receive the reply that they contribute a great deal to knowledge. 'That is true,' remarks someone, 'but their contributions are worthless and wearisome.' The reply to that is a shrug, or a change of the subject, or annoyance, or laughter, and in a little while, when you ask again, you can learn once more that they contribute to knowledge, and finally when you are asked the question you yourself will reply – if you are not careful – to the same effect. And perhaps indeed it is well not to be too obstinate, but to yield to public sentiment, to accept the extant hovering dogs, and without recognizing their right to existence, which cannot be done, yet to tolerate them. But more than this must not be required; that would be going too far, and yet the demand is made. We are perpetually being asked to put up with new hovering dogs who are always appearing. One does not even know where they come from. Do these dogs multiply by propagation? Have they actually the strength for that? – for they are nothing much more than a beautiful coat of hair, and what is there in that to propagate? But even if that improbable contingency were possible, when could it take place? For they are invariably seen alone, self-complacently floating high up in the air, and if for once in a while they descend to take a run, it lasts only for a minute or two, a few mincing struts and once more they are back in strict solitude, absorbed in what is supposed to be profound thought, from which, even when they exert themselves to the utmost, they cannot tear themselves free, or at least so they say. But if they do not propagate their kind, is it credible that there can be dogs who voluntarily give up life on the solid ground, voluntarily become hovering dogs, and merely for the sake of the comfort and a certain technical accomplishment choose that empty life on cushions up there? It is unthinkable; neither propagation nor voluntary transition is thinkable. The facts, however, show that there are always new hovering dogs in evidence; from which one must conclude that, in spite of obstacles which appear insurmountable to our understanding, no dog species, however curious, ever dies out, once it exists, or, at least, not without a tough struggle, not without being capable of putting up a successful defence for a long time.

But if that is valid for such an out-of-the-way, externally odd, inefficient species as the hovering dog, must I not also accept it as valid for mine? Besides, I am not in the least queer outwardly; an ordinary middle-class dog such as is very prevalent in this neighbourhood, at least, I am neither particularly exceptional in any way, nor particularly repellent in any way; and in my youth and to some extent also in maturity, so long as I attended to my appearance and had lots of exercise, I was actually considered a very handsome dog. My front view was particularly admired, my slim legs, the fine set of my head; but my silvery white and yellow coat, which curled only at the hair tips, was very pleasing too; in all that there was nothing strange; the only strange thing about me is my nature, yet even that, as I am always careful to remember, has its foundation in universal dog nature. Now if not even the hovering dogs live in isolation, but invariably manage to encounter their fellows somewhere or other in the great dog world, and even to conjure new generations of themselves out of nothingness, then I too can live in the confidence that I am not quite forlorn. Certainly the fate of types like mine must be a strange one, and the existence of my colleagues can never be of visible help to me, if for no other reason than that I should scarcely ever be able to recognize them. We are the dogs who are crushed by the silence, who long to break through it, literally to get a breath of fresh air; the others seem to thrive on silence: true, that is only so in appearance, as in the case of the musical dogs, who ostensibly were quite calm when they played, but in reality were in a state of intense excitement; nevertheless the illusion is very strong, one tries to make a breach in it, but it mocks every attempt. What help, then, do my colleagues find? What kind of attempts do they make to manage to go on living in spite of everything? These attempts may be of various kinds. My own bout of questioning while I was young was one. So I thought that perhaps if I associated with those who asked many questions I might find my real comrades. Well, I did so for some time, with great self-control, a self-control made necessary by the annoyance I felt when I was interrupted by perpetual questions that I mostly could not answer myself: for the only thing that concerns me is to obtain answers. Moreover, who is not eager to ask questions when he is young, and how, when so many questions are going about, are you to pick out the right questions? One question sounds like another; it is the intention that counts, but that is often hidden even from the questioner. And besides it is a peculiarity of dogs to be always asking questions, they ask them confusedly all together; it is as if in doing that they were trying to obliterate every trace of the genuine questions. No, my real colleagues are not to be found among the youthful questioners, and just as little among the old and silent, to whom I now belong. But what good are all these questions, for they have failed me completely; apparently my colleagues are cleverer dogs than I, and have recourse to other excellent methods that enable them to bear this life, methods which, nevertheless, as I can tell from my own experience, though they may perhaps help at a pinch, though they may calm, lull to rest, distract, are yet on the whole as impotent as my own, for, no matter where I look, I can see no sign of their success. I am afraid that the last thing by which I can hope to recognize my real colleagues is their success. But where, then, are my real colleagues? Yes, that is the burden of my complaint; that is the kernel of it. Where are they? Everywhere and nowhere. Perhaps my next-door neighbour, only three jumps away, is one of them; we often bark across to each other, he calls on me sometimes too, though I do not call on him. Is he my real colleague? I do not know, I certainly see no sign of it in him, but it is possible. It is possible, but all the same nothing is more improbable. When he is away I can amuse myself, drawing on my fancy, by discovering in him many things that have a suspicious resemblance to myself; but once he stands before me all my fancies become ridiculous. An old dog, a little smaller even than myself – and I am hardly medium size – brown, short-haired, with a tired hang of the head and a shuffling gait; on top of all this he trails his left hind leg behind him a little because of some disease. For a long time now I have been more intimate with him than with anybody else; I am glad to say that I can still get on tolerably well with him, and when he goes away I shout the most friendly greetings after him, though not out of affection, but in anger at myself; for if I follow him I find him just as disgusting again, slinking along there with his trailing leg and his much too low hindquarters. Sometimes it seems to me as if I were trying to humiliate myself by privately calling him my colleague. Nor in our talks does he betray any trace of similarity of thought; true, he is clever and cultured enough as these things go here, and I could learn much from him; but is it for cleverness and culture that I am looking? We converse usually about local questions, and I am astonished – my isolation has made me more clear-sighted in such matters – how much intelligence is needed even by an ordinary dog, even in average and not unfavourable circumstances, if he is to live out his life and defend himself against the greater of life's customary dangers. True, knowledge provides the rules one must follow, but even to grasp them imperfectly and in rough outline is by no means easy, and when one has actually grasped them the real difficulty still remains, namely to apply them to local conditions – here almost nobody can help, almost every hour brings new tasks, and every new patch of earth its specific problems; no one can maintain that he has settled everything for good and that henceforth his life will go on, so to speak, of itself, not even I myself, though my needs shrink literally from day to day. And all this ceaseless labour – to what end? Merely to entomb oneself deeper and deeper in silence, it seems, so deep that one can never be dragged out of it again by any-body.

People often cry up the universal progress made by the dog

community throughout the ages, and probably mean by that more particularly the progress in knowledge. Certainly knowledge is progressing, its advance is irresistible, it actually progresses at an accelerating speed, always faster, but what is there to praise in that? It is as if one were to praise someone because with the years he grows older, and in consequence comes nearer and nearer to death with increasing speed. That is a natural and moreover an ugly process in which I find nothing to praise. I can only see decline everywhere, in saying which, however, I do not mean that earlier generations were essentially better than ours, but only younger; that was their great advantage, their memory was not so overburdened as ours today, it was easier to get them to speak out, and even if nobody actually succeeded in doing that, the possibility of it was greater, and it is indeed this greater sense of possibility that moves us so deeply when we listen to those old and strangely simple stories. Here and there we catch a curiously significant phrase and we would almost like to leap to our feet, if we did not feel the weight of centuries upon us. No, whatever objection I may have to my age, former generations were not better, indeed in a sense they were far worse, far weaker. Even in those days wonders did not openly walk the streets for any one to seize; but all the same dogs – I cannot put it in any other way – had not yet become so doggish as today, the edifice of dogdom was still loosely put together, the true Word could still have intervened, planning or replanning the structure, changing it at will, transforming it into its opposite; and the Word was there, was very near at least, on the tip of everybody's tongue, anyone might have hit upon it. And what has become of it today? Today one may pluck out one's very heart and not find it. Our generation is lost, it may be, but it is more blameless than those earlier ones. I can understand the hesitation of my generation, indeed it is no longer mere hesitation; it is the thousandth forgetting of a dream dreamt a thousand times and forgotten a thousand times; and who can damn us merely for forgetting for the thousandth time? But I fancy I understand the hesitation of our forefathers too, we would probably have acted just as they did; indeed I could almost say: Well for us that it was not we who had to take the guilt upon us, that instead we can hasten in almost guiltless silence towards death in a world darkened by others. When our first fathers strayed they had doubtless scarcely any notion that their aberration was to be an endless one, they could still literally see the cross-roads, it seemed an easy matter to turn back whenever they pleased, and if they hesitated to turn back it was merely because they wanted to enjoy a dog's life for a little while longer; it was not yet a genuine dog's life, and already it seemed intoxicatingly beautiful to them, so what must it become in a little while, a very little while, and so they strayed farther. They did not know what we can now guess at, contemplating the course of history: that change begins in the soul before it appears in ordinary existence, and that, when they began to enjoy a dog's life, they must already have possessed real old dogs' souls, and were by no means so near their starting-point as they thought, or as their eyes feasting on all doggish joys tried to persuade them. But who can speak of youth at this time of day? These were the really young dogs, but their sole ambition unfortunately was to become old dogs, truly a thing which they could not fail to achieve, as all succeeding generations show, and ours, the last, most clearly of all.

Naturally I do not talk to my neighbour of these things, yet often I cannot but think of them when I am sitting opposite him – that typical old dog – or bury my nose in his coat, which already has a whiff of the smell of cast-off hides. To talk to him, or even to any of the others, about such things, would be pointless. I know what course the conversation would take. He would urge a slight objection now and then, but finally he would agree – agreement is the best weapon of defence – and the matter would be buried: why indeed trouble to exhume it at all? And in spite of this there is a profound understanding between my neighbours and me, going deeper than mere words. I shall never cease to maintain that, though I have no proof of it and perhaps am merely suffering from an ordinary delusion, caused by the fact that for a long time this dog has been the only one with whom I have held any communication, and so I am bound to cling to him. 'Are you after all my colleague in your own fashion? And ashamed because everything has miscarried with you? Look, the same fate has been mine. When I am alone I weep over it; come, it is sweeter to weep in company.' I often have such thoughts as these and then I give him a prolonged look. He does not lower his glance, but neither can one read anything from it; he gazes at me dully, wondering why I am silent and why I have broken off the conversation. But perhaps that very glance is his way of questioning me, and I disappoint him just as he disappoints me. In my youth, if other problems had not been more important to me then, and I had not been perfectly satisfied with my own company, I would probably have asked him straight out and received an answer flatly agreeing with me, and that would have been worse even than today's silence. But is not everybody silent in exactly the same way? What is there to prevent me from believing that everyone is my colleague instead of thinking that I have only one or two fellow-inquirers – lost and forgotten along with their petty achievements, so that I can never reach them by any road through the darkness of ages or the confused throng of the present: why not believe that all dogs from the beginning of time have been my colleagues, all diligent in their own way, all unsuccessful in their own way, all silent or falsely garrulous in their own way, as hopeless research is apt to make one? But in that case I need not have severed myself from my fellows at all, I could have remained quietly among the others, I had no need to fight my way out like a stubborn child through the closed ranks of the grown-ups, who indeed wanted as much as I to find a way out, and who seemed incomprehensible to me simply because of their knowledge, which told them that nobody could ever escape and that it was stupid to use force.

Such ideas, however, are definitely due to the influence of my neighbour; he confuses me, he fills me with dejection; and yet in himself he is happy enough, at least when he is in his own quarters I often hear him shouting and singing; it is really unbearable. It would be a good thing to renounce this last tie also, to cease giving way to the vague dreams which all contact with dogs unavoidably provokes, no matter how hardened one may consider oneself, and to employ the short time that still remains for me exclusively in prosecuting my researches. The next time he comes I shall slip away, or pretend I am asleep, and keep up the pretence until he stops visiting me.

Also my researches have become intermittent, I relax, I grow weary, I trot mechanically where once I raced enthusiastically, think of the time when I began to inquire into the question: 'Whence does the earth procure this food?' Then indeed I really lived among the people, I pushed my way where the crowd was thickest, wanted everybody to know my work and be my audience, and my audience was even more essential to me than my work; I still expected to produce some effect or other, and that naturally gave me a great impetus, which now that I am solitary is gone. But in those days I was so full of strength that I achieved something unprecedented, something at variance with all our principles, and that every contemporary eyewitness assuredly recalls now as an uncanny feat. Our scientific knowledge, which generally makes for an extreme specialization, is remarkably simple in one province. I mean where it teaches that the earth engenders our food, and then, after having laid down this hypothesis, gives the methods by which the different foods may be obtained in their best kinds and greatest abundance. Now it is of course true that the earth brings forth all food, of that there can be no doubt: but as simple as people generally imagine it to be the matter is not; and their belief that it is simple prevents further inquiry. Take an ordinary occurrence that happens every day. If we were to be quite inactive, as I am almost completely now, and after a perfunctory scratching and watering of the soil lay down and waited for what was to come, then we should find the food on the ground, assuming, that is, that a result of some kind is inevitable. Nevertheless that is not what usually happens. Those who have preserved even a little freedom of judgement on scientific matters – and their numbers are truly small, for science draws a wider and wider circle round itself – will easily see, without having to make any specific experiment, that the main part of the food that is discovered on the ground in such cases comes from above; indeed customarily we snap up most of our food, according to our dexterity and greed, before it has reached the ground at all. In saying that, however, I am saying nothing against science; the earth, of course, brings forth this kind of food too. Whether the earth draws one kind of food out of itself and calls down another kind from the skies perhaps makes no essential difference, and science, which has established that in both cases it is necessary to prepare the ground, need not perhaps concern itself with such distinctions, for does it not say: 'If you have food in your jaws you have solved all questions for the time being.' But it seems to me that science nevertheless takes a veiled interest, at least to some extent, in these matters, inasmuch as it recognizes two chief methods of procuring food; namely, the actual preparation of the ground, and secondly the auxiliary perfecting processes of incantation, dance, and song. I find here a distinction in accordance with the one I have myself made; not a definitive distinction, perhaps, but yet clear enough. The scratching and watering of the ground, in my opinion, serves to produce both kinds of food, and remains indispensable; incantation, dance, and song, however, are concerned less with the ground food in the narrower sense, and serve principally to attract the food from above. Tradition fortifies me in this interpretation. The ordinary dogs themselves set science right here without knowing it, and without science being able to venture a word in reply. If, as science claims, these ceremonies minister only to the soil, giving it the potency, let us say, to attract food from the air, then logically they should be directed exclusively to the soil; it is the soil that the incantations must be whispered to, the soil that must be danced to. And to the best of my knowledge science ordains nothing else than this. But now comes the remarkable thing; the people in all their ceremonies gaze upwards. This is no insult to science, since science does not forbid it, but leaves the husbandman complete freedom in this respect; in its teaching it takes only the soil into account, and if the husbandman carries out its instructions concerning the preparation of the ground it is content; yet, in my opinion, it should really demand more than this if it is logical. And, though I have never been deeply initiated into science, I simply cannot conceive how the learned can bear to let our people, unruly and passionate as they are, chant their incantations with their faces turned upwards, wail our ancient folk songs into the air, and spring high in their dances as though, forgetting the ground, they wished to take flight from it for ever. I took this contradiction as my starting-point and whenever, according to the teachings of science, the harvest time was approaching, I restricted my attention to the ground, it was the ground that I scratched in the dance, and I almost gave myself a crick in the neck keeping my head as close to the ground as I could. Later I dug a hole for my nose, and sang and declaimed into it so that only the ground might hear, and nobody else beside or above me.

The results of my experiment were meagre. Sometimes the food did not appear, and I was already preparing to rejoice at this proof, but then the food would appear; it was exactly as if my strange performance had caused some confusion at first, but had shown itself later to possess advantages, so that in my case the usual barking and leaping could be dispensed with. Often, indeed, the food appeared in greater abundance than formerly, but then again it would stay away altogether. With a diligence hitherto unknown in a young dog I drew up exact re-

ports of all my experiments, fancied that here and there I was
on a scent that might lead me further, but then it lost itself
again in obscurity. My inadequate grounding in science also
undoubtedly held me up here. What guarantee had I, for instance, that the absence of the food was not caused by un-
scientific preparation of the ground rather than by my experiments, and if that should be so, then all my conclusions were
invalid. In certain circumstances I might have been able to
achieve an almost scrupulously exact experiment: namely, if I
had succeeded only once in bringing down food by an upward
incantation without preparing the ground at all, and then had
failed to extract food by an incantation directed exclusively to
the ground. I attempted indeed something of this kind, but
without any real belief in it and without conditions being quite
perfect; for it is my fixed opinion that a certain amount of
ground-preparation is always necessary, and even if the heretics
who deny this are right, their theory can never be proved in any
case, seeing that the watering of the ground is done under a
kind of compulsion, and within certain limits simply cannot be
avoided. Another and somewhat tangential experiment succeeded better and aroused some public attention. Arguing from
the customary method of snatching food while still in the air, I
decided to allow the food to fall to the ground, but to make no
effort to snatch it. Accordingly I always made a small jump in
the air when the food appeared, but timed it so that it might
always fail of its object; in the majority of instances the food
fell dully and indifferently to the ground in spite of this, and I
flung myself furiously upon it, with the fury both of hunger
and of disappointment. But in isolated cases something else
happened, something really strange; the food did not fall but
followed me through the air; the food pursued the hungry. That
never went on for long, always for only a short stretch, then
the food fell after all, or vanished completely, or – the most common case – my greed put a premature end to the experiment and
I swallowed down the tempting bait. All the same I was happy

at that time, a stir of curiosity ran through my neighbourhood, I attracted uneasy attention, I found my acquaintances more accessible to my questions, I could see in their eyes a gleam that seemed like an appeal for help; and even if it was only the reflection of my own glance I asked for nothing more, I was satisfied. Until at last I discovered – and the others discovered it simultaneously – that this experiment of mine was a commonplace of science, had already succeeded with others far more brilliantly than with me, and though it had not been attempted for a long time on account of the extreme self-control it required, had also no need to be repeated, for scientifically it had no value at all. It only proved what was already known, that the ground not only attracts food vertically from above, but also at a slant, indeed sometimes in spirals. So there I was left with my experiment, but I was not discouraged, I was too young for that; on the contrary, this disappointment braced me to attempt perhaps the greatest achievement of my life. I did not believe the scientists' depreciations of my experiment, yet belief was of no avail here, but only proof, and I resolved to set about establishing that and thus raise my experiment from its original irrelevance and set it in the very centre of the field of research. I wished to prove that when I retreated before the food it was not the ground that attracted it at a slant, but I who drew it after me. This first experiment, it is true, I could not carry any further; to see the food before one and experiment in a scientific spirit at the same time – one cannot keep that up indefinitely. But I decided to do something else; I resolved to fast completely as long as I could stand it, and at the same time avoid all sight of food, all temptation. If I were to withdraw myself in this manner, remain lying day and night with closed eyes, trouble myself neither to snatch food from the air nor to lift it from the ground, and if, as I dared not expect, yet faintly hoped, without taking any of the customary measures, and merely in response to the unavoidable irrational watering of the ground and the quiet recitation of the incantations and songs (the dance I wished to omit, so as not to weaken my powers) the food were to come of itself from above, and without going near the ground were to knock at my teeth for admittance – if that were to happen, then, even if science was not confuted, for it has enough elasticity to admit exceptions and isolated cases – I asked myself what would the other dogs say, who fortunately do not possess such extreme elasticity? For this would be no exceptional case like those handed down by history, such as the incident, let us say, of the dog who refuses, because of bodily illness or trouble of mind, to prepare the ground, to track down and seize his food, upon which the whole dog community recite magical formulae and by this means succeed in making the food deviate from its customary route into the jaws of the invalid. I, on the contrary, was perfectly sound and at the height of my powers, my appetite so splendid that it prevented me all day from thinking of anything but itself; I submitted, moreover, whether it be credited or not, voluntarily to my period of fasting, was myself quite able to conjure down my own supply of food and wished also to do so, and so I asked no assistance from the dog community, and indeed rejected it in the most determined manner.

I sought a suitable place for myself in an outlying clump of bushes, where I would have to listen to no talk of food, no sound of munching jaws and bones being gnawed; I ate my fill for the last time and laid me down. As far as possible I wanted to pass my whole time with closed eyes; until the food came it would be perpetual night for me, even though my vigil might last for days or weeks. During that time, however, I dared not sleep much, better indeed if I did not sleep at all – and that made everything much harder – for I must not only conjure the food down from the air, but also be on my guard lest I should be asleep when it arrived; yet on the other hand sleep would be very welcome to me, for I would manage to fast much longer asleep than awake. For those reasons I decided to arrange my time prudently and sleep a great deal, but always in short snatches. I achieved this by always resting my head while I slept on some frail twig, which soon snapped and so awoke me. So there I lay, sleeping or keeping watch, dreaming or singing quietly to myself. My first vigils passed uneventfully; perhaps in the place whence the food came no one had yet noticed that I was lying there in resistance to the normal course of things, and so there was no sign. I was a little disturbed in my concentration by the fear that the other dogs might miss me, presently find me, and attempt something or other against me. A second fear was that at the mere wetting of the ground, though it was unfruitful ground according to the findings of science, some chance nourishment might appear and seduce me by its smell. But for a time nothing of that kind happened and I could go on fasting. Apart from such fears I was more calm during this first stage than I could remember ever having been before. Although in reality I was labouring to annul the findings of science, I felt within me a deep reassurance, indeed almost the proverbial serenity of the scientific worker. In my thoughts I begged forgiveness of science; there must be room in it for my researches too; consolingly in my ears rang the assurance that no matter how great the effect of my inquiries might be, and indeed the greater the better, I would not be lost to ordinary dog life; science regarded my attempts with benevolence, it itself would undertake the interpretation of my discoveries, and that promise already meant fulfilment; while until now I had felt outlawed in my innermost heart and had run my head against the traditional walls of my species like a savage, I would now be accepted with great honour, the long-yearned-for warmth of assembled canine bodies would lap me round, I would ride uplifted high on the shoulders of my fellows. Remarkable effects of my first hunger. My achievement seemed so great to me that I began to weep with emotion and self-pity there among the quiet bushes, which it must be confessed was not very understandable, for when I was looking forward to my well-earned reward why should I weep? Probably out of pure happiness. It is always when I am happy, and that is seldom enough, that I weep. After that, however, these feelings soon passed. My beautiful fancies fled one by one before the increasing urgency of my hunger; a little longer and I was, after an abrupt farewell to all my imaginations and my sublime feelings, totally alone with the hunger burning in my entrails. 'That is my hunger,' I told myself countless times during this stage, as if I wanted to convince myself that my hunger and I were still two things and I could shake it off like a burdensome lover; but in reality we were very painfully one, and when I explained to myself: 'That is my hunger,' it was really my hunger that was speaking and having its joke at my expense. A bad, bad time! I still shudder to think of it, and not merely, please note this, on account of the suffering I endured then, but because I know I was insufficiently equipped then and consequently shall have to live through that suffering once more if I am ever to achieve anything; for today I still hold fasting to be the final and most potent weapon of research. The way goes through fasting; the highest, if it is attainable, is attainable only by the highest effort, and the highest effort among us is voluntary fasting. So when I think of those times – and I would gladly pass my life in brooding over them – I cannot help thinking also of the time that still threatens me. It seems to me that it takes almost a lifetime to recuperate from such an attempt; my whole life as an adult lies between me and that fast, and I have not recovered yet. When I begin upon my next fast I shall perhaps have more resolution than the first time, because of my greater experience and deeper insight into the need for the attempt, but my powers are still enfeebled by that first essay, and so I shall probably begin to fail at the mere approach of these familiar horrors. My weaker appetite will not help me; it will reduce the value of the attempt only by a very little, and will, indeed, probably force me to fast longer than was necessary the first time. I think I am clear on these and many other matters, the long interval has not been wanting in trial attempts, often enough I have literally got my teeth into hunger; but I was still not strong enough for the ultimate effort, and now the unspoilt ardour of youth is of course gone for ever. It vanished in the great privations of that first fast. All sorts of thoughts tormented me. Our forefathers appeared threateningly before me. True, I held them responsible for everything, even if I dared not say so openly; it was they who involved our dog life in guilt, and so I could easily have responded to their menaces with counter-menaces; but I bow before their knowledge, it came from sources of which we know no longer, and for that reason, much as I may feel compelled to oppose them, I shall never actually overstep their laws, but content myself with wriggling out through the gaps, for which I have a particularly good nose. On the question of fasting I appealed to the well-known dialogue in the course of which one of our sages once expressed the intention of forbidding fasting, but was dissuaded by a second with the words: 'But who would ever think of fasting?' whereupon the first sage allowed himself to be persuaded and withdrew the prohibition. But now arises the question: 'Is not fasting really forbidden after all?' The great majority of commentators deny this and regard fasting as freely permitted, and holding as they think with the second sage do not worry in the least about the evil consequences that may result from erroneous interpretations. I had naturally assured myself on this point before I began my fast. But now that I was twisted with the pangs of hunger, and in my distress of mind sought relief in my own hind legs, despairingly licking and gnawing at them up to the very buttocks, the universal interpretation of this dialogue seemed to me entirely and completely false, I cursed the commentators' science, I cursed myself for having been led astray by it; for the dialogue contained, as any child could see, more than merely one prohibition of fasting; the first sage wished to forbid fasting; what a sage wishes is already done, so fasting was forbidden; as for the second sage, he not only agreed with the first, but actually considered fasting impossible, piled therefore on the first prohibition a second, that of dog nature itself; the first sage saw this and thereupon withdrew the explicit prohibition, that was to say, he imposed upon all dogs, the matter being now settled, the obligation to know themselves and to make their own prohibitions regarding fasting. So here was a threefold prohibition instead of merely one, and I had violated it. Now I could at least have obeyed at this point, though tardily, but in the midst of pain I felt a longing to go on fasting, and I followed it as greedily as if it were a strange dog. I could not stop; perhaps too I was already too weak to get up and seek safety for myself in familiar scenes. I tossed about on the fallen forest leaves, I could no longer sleep, I heard noises on every side; the world, which had been asleep during my life hitherto, seemed to have been awakened by my fasting, I was tortured by the fancy that I would never be able to eat again, and I must eat so as to reduce to silence this world rioting so noisily round me, and I would never be able to do so; but the greatest noise of all came from my own belly, I often laid my ear against it with startled eyes, for I could hardly believe what I heard. And now that things were becoming unendurable my very nature seemed to be seized by the general frenzy, and made senseless attempts to save itself; the smell of food began to assail me, delicious dainties that I had long since forgotten, delights of my childhood; yes, I could smell the very fragrance of my mother's teats; I forgot my resolution to resist all smells, or rather I did not forget it; I dragged myself to and fro, never for more than a few yards, and sniffed as if that were in accordance with my resolution, as if I were looking for food simply to be on my guard against it. The fact that I found nothing did not disappoint me; the food must be there, only it was always a few steps away, my legs failed me before I could reach it. But simultaneously I knew that nothing was there, and that I made those feeble movements simply out of fear lest I might collapse in this place and never be able to leave it. My last hopes, my last dreams vanished; I would perish here miserably; of what use were my researches? – childish attempts undertaken in childish and far happier days; here and now was the hour of deadly earnest, here my inquiries should have shown their value, but where had they vanished? Only a dog lay here helplessly snapping at the empty air, a dog who, though he still watered the ground with convulsive haste at short intervals and without being aware of it, could not remember even the shortest of the countless incantations stored in his memory, not even the little rhyme which the newly born puppy says when it snuggles under its mother. It seemed to me as if I were separated from all my fellows not by a quite short stretch, but by an infinite distance, and as if I would die less of hunger than of neglect. For it was clear that nobody troubled about me, nobody beneath the earth, on it, or above it; I was dying of their indifference; they said indifferently: 'He is dying,' and it would actually come to pass. And did I not myself assent? Did I not say the same thing? Had I not wanted to be forsaken like this? Yes, brothers, but not so as to perish in that place, but to achieve truth and escape from this world of falsehood, where there is no one from whom you can learn the truth, not even from me, born as I am a citizen of falsehood. Perhaps the truth was not so very far off, and I not so forsaken, therefore, as I thought; or I may have been forsaken less by my fellows than by myself, in yielding and consenting to die.

But one does not die so easily as a nervous dog imagines. I merely fainted, and when I came to and raised my eyes a strange hound was standing before me. I did not feel hungry, but rather filled with strength, and my limbs, it seemed to me, were light and agile, though I made no attempt to prove this by getting to my feet. My visual faculties in themselves were no keener than usual; a beautiful but not at all extraordinary hound stood before me; I could see that, and that was all, and yet it seemed to me that I saw something more in him. There was blood under me, at first I took it for food; but I recognized it immediately as blood that I had vomited. I turned my eyes from it to the strange hound. He was lean, long-legged, brown with a patch of white here and there, and had a fine, strong, piercing glance. 'What are you doing here?' he asked. 'You must leave this place.' 'I can't leave it just now,' I said, without trying to explain, for how could I explain everything to him; besides, he seemed to be in a hurry. 'Please go away,' he said, impatiently lifting his feet and setting them down again. 'Let me be,' I said, 'leave me to myself and don't worry about me; the others don't.' 'I ask you to go for your own sake,' he said. 'You can ask for any reason you like,' I replied. 'I can't go even if I wanted to.' 'You need have no fear of that,' he said, smiling. 'You can go all right. It's because you seem to be feeble that I ask you to go now, and you can go slowly if you like; if you linger now you'll have to race off later on.' 'That's my affair,' I replied. 'It's mine too,' he said, saddened by my stubbornness, yet obviously resolved to let me lie for the time being, but at the same time to seize the opportunity of paying court to me. At any other time I would gladly have submitted to the blandishments of such a beautiful creature, but at that moment, why, I cannot tell, the thought filled me with terror. 'Get out!' I screamed, and all the louder as I had no other means of protecting myself. 'All right, I'll leave you then,' he said, slowly retreating. 'You're wonderful. Don't I please you?' 'You'll please me by going away and leaving me in peace,' I said, but I was no longer so sure of myself as I tried to make him think. My senses, sharpened by fasting, suddenly seemed to see or hear something about him; it was just beginning, it was growing, it came nearer, and I knew that this hound had the power to drive me away, even if I could not imagine to myself at the moment how I was ever to get to my feet. And I gazed at him – he had merely shaken his head sadly at my rough answer – with ever-mounting desire. 'Who are you?' I asked. 'I'm a hunter,' he replied. 'And why won't you let me lie here?' I asked. 'You disturb me,' he said. 'I can't hunt while you're here.' 'Try,' I said, 'perhaps you'll be able to hunt after all.' 'No,' he said, 'I'm sorry, but you must go.' 'Don't hunt for this one day!' I implored him. 'No,' he said, 'I must hunt.' 'I must go; you must hunt,' I said, 'nothing but musts. Can you explain to me why we must?' 'No,' replied he, 'but there's nothing that needs to be explained, these are natural, self-evident things.' 'Not quite self-evident as all that,' I said, 'you're sorry that you must drive me away, and yet you do it.' 'That's so,' he replied. 'That's so,' I echoed him crossly, 'that isn't an answer. Which sacrifice would you rather make: to give up your hunting or give up driving me away?' 'To give up my hunting,' he said without hesitation. 'There!' said I, 'don't you see that you're contradicting yourself?' 'How am I contradicting myself?' he replied. 'My dear little dog, can it be that you really don't understand that I must? Don't you understand the most self-evident fact?' I made no answer, for I noticed – a new life ran through me, life such as terror gives – I noticed from almost invisible indications, which perhaps nobody but myself could have noticed, that in the depths of his chest the hound was preparing to upraise a song. 'You're going to sing,' I said. 'Yes,' he replied gravely, 'I'm going to sing, soon, but not yet.' 'You're beginning already,' I said. 'No,' he said, 'not yet. But be prepared.' 'I can hear it already, though you deny it,' I said, trembling. He was silent, and then I thought I saw something such as no dog before me had ever seen, at least there is no slightest hint of it in our tradition, and I hastily bowed my head in infinite fear and shame in the pool of blood lying before me. I thought I saw that the hound was already singing without knowing it, nay, more, that the melody, separated from him, was floating on the air in accordance with its own laws, and, as though he had no part in it, was moving towards me, towards me alone. Today, of course, I deny the validity of all such perceptions and ascribe them to my over-excitation at that time, but even if it was an error it had nevertheless a sort of grandeur, and is the sole, even if delusive reality that I have carried over into this world from my period of fasting, and shows at least how far we can go when we are beyond ourselves. And I was actually quite beyond myself. In ordinary circumstances I would have been very ill, incapable of moving; but the melody, which the hound soon seemed to acknowledge as his, was quite irresistible. It grew stronger and stronger; its waxing power seemed to have no limits, and already almost burst my ear-drums. But the worst was that it seemed to exist solely for my sake, this voice before whose sublimity the woods fell silent to exist solely for my sake; who was I, that I could dare to remain here, lying brazenly before it in my pool of blood and filth. I tottered to my feet and looked down at myself; this wretched body can never run, I still had time to think, but already, spurred on by the melody, I was careering from the spot in splendid style. I said nothing to my friends; probably I could have told them all when I first arrived, but I was too feeble, and later it seemed to me that such things could not be told. Hints which I could not refrain from occasionally dropping were quite lost in the general conversation. For the rest I recovered physically in a few hours, but spiritually I still suffer from the effects of that experiment.

Nevertheless, I next carried my researches into music. True, science had not been idle in this sphere either; the science of music, if I am correctly informed, is perhaps still more comprehensive than that of nurture, and in any case established on a firmer basis. That may be explained by the fact that this province admits of more objective inquiry than the other, and its knowledge is more a matter of pure observation and systematization, while in the province of food the main object is to achieve practical results. That is the reason why the science of music is accorded greater esteem than that of nurture, but also why the former has never penetrated so deeply into the life of the people. I myself felt less attracted to the science of music than to any other until I heard that voice in the forest. My experience with the musical dogs had indeed drawn my attention to music, but I was still too young at that time. Nor is it by any means easy even to come to grips with that science; it is regarded as very esoteric and politely excludes the crowd. Besides, although what struck me most deeply at first about these dogs was their music, their silence seemed to me still more significant; as for their affrighting music, probably it was quite unique, so that I could leave it out of account; but thenceforth their silence confronted me everywhere and in all the dogs I met. So for penetrating into real dog nature research into food seemed to me the best method, calculated to lead me to my goal by the straightest path. Perhaps I was mistaken. A border region between these two sciences, however, had already attracted my attention. I mean the theory of incantation, by which food is called down. Here again it is very much against me that I have never seriously tackled the science of music and in this sphere cannot even count myself among the half-educated, the class on whom science looks down most of all. This fact I cannot get away from. I could not – I have proof of that, unfortunately – I could not pass even the most elementary scientific examination set by an authority on the subject. Of course, quite apart from the circumstances already mentioned, the reason for that can be found in my incapacity for scientific investigation, my limited powers of thought, my bad memory, but above all in my inability to keep my scientific aim continuously before my eyes. All this I frankly admit, even with a certain degree of pleasure. For the more profound cause of my scientific incapacity seems to me to be an instinct, and indeed by no means a bad one. If I wanted to brag I might say that it was this very instinct that invalidated my scientific capacities, for it would surely be a very extraordinary thing if one who shows a tolerable degree of intelligence in dealing with the ordinary daily business of life, which certainly cannot be called simple, and moreover one whose findings have been checked and verified, where that was possible, by individual scientists if not by science itself, should a *priori* be incapable of planting his paw even on the first rung of the ladder of science. It was this instinct that made me – and perhaps for the sake of science it-self, but a different science from that of today, an ultimate science – prize freedom higher than everything else. Freedom! Certainly such freedom as is possible today is a wretched business. But nevertheless freedom, nevertheless a possession.

The Burrow

I HAVE completed the construction of my burrow and it seems to be successful. All that can be seen from the outside is a big hole; that, however, really leads nowhere; if you take a few steps you strike against natural firm rock. I can make no boast of having contrived this ruse intentionally; it is simply the remains of one of my many abortive building attempts, but finally it seemed to me advisable to leave this one hole without filling it in. True, some ruses are so subtle that they defeat themselves, I know that better than anyone, and it is certainly a risk to draw attention by this hole to the fact that there may be something in the vicinity worth inquiring into. But you do not know me if you think I am afraid, or that I built my burrow simply out of fear. At a distance of some thousand paces from this hole lies, covered by a movable layer of moss, the real entrance to the burrow; it is secured as safely as anything in this world can be secured; yet someone could step on the moss or break through it, and then my burrow would lie open, and anybody who liked – please note, however, that quite uncommon abilities would also be required – could make his way in and utterly destroy everything. I know that very well, and even now when I am better off than ever before I can scarcely pass an hour in complete tranquillity; at that one point in the dark moss I am vulnerable, and in my dreams I often see a greedy muzzle sniffing round it persistently. It will be objected that I could quite well have filled in the entrance too, with a thin layer of hard earth on top and with loose soil further down, so that it would not cost me much trouble to dig my way out again whenever I liked. But that plan is impossible; prudence itself demands that I should have a way of leaving at a moment's notice if necessary, prudence itself demands, as alas! so often, the element of risk in life. All this involves very laborious

calculation, and the sheer pleasure of the mind in its own keen-
ness is often the sole reason why one keeps it up. I must have a
way of leaving at a moment's notice, for, despite all my vigilance, may I not be attacked from some quite unexpected
quarter? I live in peace in the inmost chamber of my house, and
meanwhile the enemy may be burrowing his way slowly and
stealthily towards me. I do not say that he has a better scent
than I; probably he knows as little about me as I of him. But
there are insatiable robbers who burrow blindly through the
ground, and to whom the very size of my house gives the hope
of hitting by chance on some of its far-flung passages. I certainly have the advantage of being in my own house and knowing all the passages and how they run. A robber may very
easily become my victim and a succulent one too. But I am
growing old; I am not as strong as many others, and my enemies
are countless; it could well happen that in flying from one
enemy I might run into the jaws of another. Anything might
happen! In any case I must have the confident knowledge that
somewhere there is an exit easy to reach and quite free, where
I have to do nothing whatever to get out, so that I might
never – Heaven shield us! – suddenly feel the teeth of the pur-
suer in my flank while I am desperately burrowing away, even
if it is at loose easy soil. And it is not only by external enemies
that I am threatened. There are also enemies in the bowels of
the earth. I have never seen them, but legend tells of them and
I firmly believe in them. They are creatures of the inner earth;
not even legend can describe them. Their very victims can
scarcely have seen them; they come, you hear the scratching of
their claws just under you in the ground, which is their element,
and already you are lost. Here it is of no avail to console yourself with the thought that you are in your own house; far
rather are you in theirs. Not even my exit could save me from
them; indeed in all probability it would not save me in any
case, but rather betray me; yet it is a hope, and I cannot live
without it. Apart from this main exit I am also connected with

the outer world by quite narrow, tolerably safe passages which provide me with good fresh air to breathe. They are the work of the field mice. I have made judicious use of them, transforming them into an organic part of my burrow. They also give me the possibility of scenting things from afar, and thus serve as a protection. All sorts of small fry, too, come running through them, and I devour these; so I can have a certain amount of subterranean hunting, sufficient for a modest way of life, without leaving my burrow at all; and that is naturally a great advantage.

But the most beautiful thing about my burrow is the stillness. Of course, that is deceptive. At any moment it may be shattered and then all will be over. For the time being, however, the silence is still with me. For hours I can stroll through my passages and hear nothing except the rustling of some little creature, which I immediately reduce to silence between my jaws, or the pattering of soil, which draws my attention to the need for repair; otherwise all is still. The fragrance of the woods floats in; the place feels both warm and cool. Sometimes I lie down and roll about in the passage with pure joy. When autumn sets in, to possess a burrow like mine, and a roof over your head, is great good fortune for anyone getting on in years. Every hundred yards I have widened the passages into little round cells; there I can curl myself up in comfort and lie warm. There I sleep the sweet sleep of tranquillity, of satisfied desire, of achieved ambition; for I possess a house. I do not know whether it is a habit that still persists from former days, or whether the perils even of this house of mine are great enough to awaken me; but invariably every now and then I start up out of profound sleep and listen, listen into the stillness which reigns here unchanged day and night, smile contentedly and then sink with loosened limbs into still profounder sleep. Poor homeless wanderers in the roads and woods, creeping for warmth into a heap of leaves or a herd of their comrades, delivered into all the perils of heaven and earth! I lie here in a room secured on every side – there are more than fifty such rooms in my burrow – and pass as much time as I choose between dozing and unconscious sleep.

Not quite in the centre of the burrow, carefully chosen to serve as a refuge in case of extreme danger from siege if not from immediate pursuit, lies the chief cell. While all the rest of the burrow is the outcome rather of intense intellectual than of physical labour, this Castle Keep was fashioned by the most arduous labour of my whole body. Several times, in the despair brought on by physical exhaustion, I was on the point of giving up the whole business, flung myself down panting and cursed the burrow, dragged myself outside and left the place lying open to all the world. I could afford to do that, for I had no longer any wish to return to it, until at last, after hours or days, back I went repentantly, and when I saw that the burrow was unharmed I could almost have raised a hymn of thanksgiving, and in sincere gladness of heart started on the work anew. My labours on the Castle Keep were also made harder, and unnecessarily so (unnecessarily in that the burrow derived no real benefit from those labours) by the fact that just at the place where, according to my calculations, the Castle Keep should be, the soil was very loose and sandy and had literally to be hammered and pounded into a firm state to serve as a wall for the beautifully vaulted chamber. But for such tasks the only tool I possess is my forehead. So I had to run with my forehead thousands and thousands of times, for whole days and nights, against the ground, and I was glad when the blood came, for that was a proof that the walls were beginning to harden; and in that way, as everybody must admit, I richly paid for my Castle Keep.

In the Castle Keep I assemble my stores; everything over and above my daily wants that I capture inside the burrow, and everything I bring back with me from my hunting expeditions outside, I pile up here. The place is so spacious that food for half a year scarcely fills it. Consequently I can divide up my stores, walk about among them, play with them, enjoy their plenty and their various smells, and reckon up exactly how much they represent. That done, I can always arrange accordingly, and make my calculations and hunting plans for the future, taking into account the season of the year. There are times when I am so well provided for that in my indifference to food I never even touch the smaller fry that scuttle about the burrow, which, however, is probably imprudent of me. My constant preoccupation with defensive measures involves a frequent alteration or modification, though within narrow limits, of my views on how the building can best be organized for that end. Then it sometimes seems risky to make the Castle Keep the basis of defence; the ramifications of the burrow present me with manifold possibilities, and it seems more in accordance with prudence to divide up my stores somewhat, and put part of them in certain of the smaller rooms; thereupon I mark off every third room, let us say, as a reserve storeroom, or every fourth room as a main and every second as an auxiliary storeroom, and so forth. Or I ignore certain passages altogether and store no food in them, so as to throw any enemy off the scent, or I choose quite at random a very few rooms according to their distance from the main exit. Each of these new plans involves of course heavy work; I have to make my calculations and then carry my stores to their new places. True, I can do that at my leisure and without any hurry, and it is not at all unpleasant to carry such good food in your jaws, to lie down and rest whenever you like, and, which is an actual pleasure, to have an occasional nibble. But it is not so pleasant when, as sometimes happens, you suddenly fancy, starting up from your sleep, that the present distribution of your stores is completely and totally wrong, capable of leading to great dangers, and must be set right at once, no matter how tired or sleepy you may be; then I rush, then I fly, then I have no time for calculation; as I am burning to execute my perfectly new, perfectly satisfactory plan, I seize whatever my teeth hit upon and drag it or carry it away, sighing, groaning, stumbling, and nothing will content me but some radical alteration of the present state of things, which seems imminently dangerous. Until little by little full wakefulness sobers me, and I can hardly understand my panic haste, breathe in deeply the tranquillity of my house, which I myself have disturbed, return to my resting-place, fall asleep at once in new-won exhaustion, and on awakening find hanging from my jaws, say, a rat, as indubitable proof of night labours which already seem almost unreal. Then again there are times when the storing of all my food in one place seems the best plan of all. Of what use to me could my stores in the smaller rooms be, how much could I store there in any case? And whatever I put there would block the passage, and be a greater hindrance than help to me if I were pursued and had to fly. Besides, it is stupid but true that one's self-conceit suffers if one cannot see all one's stores together, and so at one glance know how much one possesses. And in dividing up my food in those various ways might not a great deal get lost? I can't be always scouring through all my passages and cross-passages so as to make sure that everything is in order. The idea of dividing up my stores is of course a good one, but only if one had several rooms similar to my Castle Keep. Several such rooms! Indeed! And who is to build them? In any case they could not be worked into the general plan of my burrow at this late stage. But I will admit that that is a fault in my burrow; it is always a fault to have only one model of anything. And I confess too that during the whole time I was constructing the burrow a vague divination that I should have more than one keep stirred in my mind, vaguely, yet clearly enough if I had only welcomed it; I did not yield to it, I felt too feeble for the enormous labour it would involve, more, I felt too feeble even to admit to myself the necessity for that labour, and comforted myself as best I could with the vague hope that a building which in any other case would clearly be inadequate, would in my own unique, exceptional, favoured case suffice, presumably, because providence was interested in the preservation of my forehead, that unique instrument. So I have only one Castle Keep, but my dark premonitions that one would not suffice have faded. However that may be I must content myself with the one big chamber, the smaller ones are simply no substitute for it, and so, when this conviction has grown on me, I begin once more to haul all my stores back from them to the Castle Keep. For some time afterwards I find a certain comfort in having all the passages and rooms free, in seeing my stores growing in the Castle Keep and emitting their variegated and mingled smells, each of which delights me in its own fashion, and every one of which I can distinguish even at a distance, as far as the very remotest passages. Then I usually enjoy periods of particular tranquillity, in which I change my sleeping-place by stages, always working in towards the centre of the burrow, always steeping myself more profoundly in the mingled smells, until at last I can no longer restrain myself and one night rush into the Castle Keep, mightily fling myself upon my stores, and glut myself with the best that I can seize until I am completely gorged. Happy, but dangerous hours; anyone who knew how to exploit them could destroy me with ease and without any risk. Here too the absence of a second or third large storeroom works to my detriment; for it is the single huge accumulated mass of food that seduces me. I try to guard myself in various ways against this danger; the distribution of my stores in the smaller rooms is really one of these expedients; but unfortunately, like other such expedients, it leads through renunciation to still greater greed, which, overruling my intelligence, makes me arbitrarily alter my plans of defence to suit its ends.

To regain my composure after such lapses I make a practice of reviewing the burrow, and after the necessary improvements have been carried out, frequently leave it, though only for a short spell. At such moments the hardship of renouncing it for a long time seems too punitive, even to myself, yet I recognize clearly the need for my occasional short excursions. It is always with a certain solemnity that I approach the exit again. During my spells of home life I avoid it, steer clear even of the outer windings of the corridor that leads to it; besides, it is no easy job to wander about there, for I have contrived there a whole little maze of passages; it was there that I began my burrow, at a time when I had no hope of ever completing it according to my plans; I began, half in play, at that corner, and so my first joy in labour found riotous satisfaction there in a labyrinthine burrow which at the time seemed to me the crown of all burrows, but which I judge today, perhaps with more justice, to be too much of an idle *tour de force*, not really worthy of the rest of the burrow, and though perhaps theoretically brilliant – here is my main entrance, I said in those days, ironically addressing my invisible enemies and seeing them all already caught and stifled in the outer labyrinth – is in reality a flimsy piece of jugglery that would hardly withstand a serious attack or the struggles of an enemy fighting for his life. Should I reconstruct this part of my burrow? I keep on postponing the decision, and the labyrinth will probably remain as it is. Apart from the sheer hard work that I should have to face, the task would also be the most dangerous imaginable. When I began the burrow I could work away at it in comparative peace of mind, the risk wasn't much greater than any other risk; but to attempt that today would be to draw the whole world's attention, and gratuitously, to my burrow; today the whole thing is impossible. I am almost glad of that, for I still have a certain sentiment about this first achievement of mine. And if a serious attack were attempted, could any kind of entrance design save me? An entrance can deceive, can lead astray, can give the attacker no end of worry, and the present one too can do that at a pinch. But a really serious attack has to be met by an instantaneous mobilization of all the resources in the burrow and all the forces of my body and soul – that, of course, is self-evident. So this entrance can very well remain where it is. The burrow has so many unavoidable defects imposed by natural causes that it can surely stand this one defect for which I am responsible, and which I recognize as a defect, even if only after the event. In spite of that, however, I do not deny that this fault worries me from time to time, indeed always. If on my customary rounds I avoid this part of the burrow, the fundamental reason is because the sight of it is painful to me, because I don't want to be perpetually reminded of a defect in my house, even if that defect is only too disturbingly present in my mind. Let it continue to exist ineradicably at the entrance; I can at least refuse to look at it as long as that is possible. If I merely walk in the direction of the entrance, even though I may be separated from it by several passages and rooms, I find myself sensing an atmosphere of great danger, actually as if my hair were growing thin and in a moment might fly off and leave me bare and shivering, exposed to the howls of my enemies. Yes, the mere thought of the entrance door brings such feelings with it, yet it is the labyrinth leading up to it that torments me most of all. Sometimes I dream that I have reconstructed it, transformed it completely, quickly, in a night, with a giant's strength, nobody having noticed, and now it is impregnable; the nights in which such dreams come to me are the sweetest I know, tears of joy and deliverance still glisten on my beard when I awaken.

So I must thread the tormenting complications of this labyrinth physically as well as mentally whenever I go out, and I am both exasperated and touched when, as sometimes happens, I lose myself for a moment in my own maze, and the work of my hands seems to be still doing its best to prove its sufficiency to me, its maker, whose final judgement has long since been passed on it. But then I find myself beneath the mossy covering, which has been left untouched for so long – since I stay for long spells in my house – that it has grown fast to the soil round it, and now only a little push with my head is needed and I am in the upper world. For a long time I do not dare to make that little movement, and if it were not that I should have to traverse the labyrinth once more I would certainly leave the matter for the time being and turn back again. Just think. Your house is protected and self-sufficient. You live in peace, warm, well-nourished, master, sole master of all your manifold passages and rooms, and all this you are prepared, it appears, not merely to give up, but actually to abandon; you nurse the confident hope, certainly, that you will regain it again; yet is it not a dangerous, a far too dangerous stake that you are playing for? Can there be any reasonable grounds for such a step? No, for such acts as these there can be no reasonable grounds. But all the same I then cautiously raise the trap-door and slip outside, let it softly fall back again, and fly as fast as I can from the treacherous spot.

Yet I am not really free. True, I am no longer confined by narrow passages, but rush through the open woods, and feel new powers awakening in my body for which there was no room, as it were, in the burrow, not even in the Castle Keep, though it had been ten times as big. The food too is better up here; though hunting is more difficult, success more rare, the results are more valuable from every point of view; I do not deny all this; I appreciate it and take advantage of it as fully as most animals, and probably more fully, for I do not hunt like a vagrant out of mere idleness or desperation, but calmly and methodically. Also I am not permanently doomed to this free life, for I know that my term is measured, that I do not have to hunt here for ever, and that, whenever I am weary of this life and wish to leave it, Someone, whose invitation I shall not be able to withstand, will, so to speak, summon me to him. And so I can pass my time here quite without care and in complete enjoyment, or rather I could, and yet I cannot. My burrow takes up too much of my thoughts. I fled from the entrance fast enough, but soon I am back at it again. I seek out a good hiding-place and keep watch on the entrance of my house – this time from outside – for whole days and nights. Call it foolish if you like; it gives me infinite pleasure and reassures me. At such times it is as if I were not so much looking at my house as at myself sleeping, and had the joy of being in a profound slumber and simultaneously of keeping vigilant guard over myself. I am privileged, as it were, not only to dream about the spectres of the night in all the helplessness and blind trust of sleep, but also at the same time to confront them in actuality with the calm judgement of the fully awake. And strangely enough I discover that my situation is not so bad as I had often thought, and will probably think again when I return to my house. In this respect – it may be in others too, but in this one especially – these excursions of mine are truly indispensable. Carefully as I have chosen an out-of-the-way place for my door, the traffic that passes it is nevertheless, if one takes a week's observations, very great; but so it is, no doubt, in all inhabited regions, and probably it is actually better to hazard risks of dense traffic, whose very impetus carries it past, than to be delivered in complete solitude to the first persistently searching intruder. Here enemies are numerous and their allies and accomplices still more numerous, but they fight one another, and while thus employed rush past my burrow without noticing it. In all my time I have never seen any one investigating the actual door of my house, which is fortunate both for me and for him, for I would certainly have launched myself at his throat, forgetting everything else in my anxiety for the burrow. True, intruders come in whose neighbourhood I dare not remain, and from whom I have to fly as soon as I scent them in the distance; on their attitude to the burrow I really can't pronounce with certainty, but it is at least a reassurance that when I presently return I never find any of them there, and the entrance is undamaged. There have been happy periods in which I could almost assure myself that the enmity of the world towards me had ceased or been assuaged, or that the strength of the burrow had raised me above the destructive struggle of former times. The burrow has probably protected me in more ways than I thought or dared think while I was inside it. This fancy used to have such a hold over me that sometimes I have been seized by the childish desire never to return to the burrow again, but to settle down somewhere close to the entrance, to pass my life watching it, and gloat perpetually upon the reflection – and in that find my happiness – how steadfast a protection my burrow would be if I were inside it. Well, one is soon roughly awakened from childish dreams. What does this protection which I am looking at here from the outside amount to after all? Dare I estimate the danger which I run inside the burrow from observations which I make when outside? Can my enemies, to begin with, have any proper awareness of me if I am not in my burrow? A certain awareness of me they certainly have, but not full awareness. And is not that full awareness the real definition of a state of danger? So the experiments I attempt here are only half-experiments or even less, calculated merely to reassure my fears and by giving me false reassurance to lay me open to great perils. No, I do not watch over my own sleep, as I imagined; rather it is I who sleep, while the destroyer watches. Perhaps he is one of those who pass the entrance without seeming to notice it, concerned merely to ascertain, just like myself, that the door is still untouched and waits for their attack, and only pass because they know that the master of the house is out, or because they are quite aware that he is guilelessly lying on the watch in the bushes close by. And I leave my post of observation and find I have had enough of this outside life; I feel that there is nothing more that I can learn here, either now or at any time. And I long to say a last good-bye to everything up here, to go down into my burrow never to return again, let things take their course, and not try to retard them with my profitless vigils. But after watching for such a long time everything that happens round the entrance, I find great difficulty in summoning the resolution to carry out the actual descent, which might easily draw anyone's attention, and without knowing what is happening behind my back and behind the door after it is fastened. I take advantage of stormy nights to get over the necessary preliminaries, and quickly bundle in my spoil; that seems to have come off, but whether it has really come off will only be known when I myself have made the descent; it will be known, but not by me, or possibly by me but then too late. So I give up the attempt and do not make the descent. I dig an experimental burrow, naturally at a good distance from the real entrance, a burrow just as long as myself, and seal it also with a covering of moss. I creep into my hole, close it after me, wait patiently, keep vigil for long or short spells, and at various hours of the day, then fling off the moss, issue from my hole, and summarize my observations. These are extremely heterogeneous, and both good and bad; but I have never been able to discover a universal principle or an infallible method of descent. In consequence of all this I have not yet summoned the resolution to make my actual descent, and am thrown into despair at the necessity of doing it soon. I almost screw myself to the point of deciding to emigrate to distant parts and take up my old comfortless life again, which had no security whatever, but was one indiscriminate succession of perils, yet in consequence prevented me from perceiving and fearing particular perils, as I am constantly reminded by comparing my secure burrow with ordinary life. Certainly such a decision would be an arrant piece of folly, produced simply by living too long in senseless freedom; the burrow is still mine, I have only to take a single step and I am safe. And I tear myself free from all my doubts and by broad daylight rush to the door, quite resolved to raise it now; but I cannot, I rush past it and fling myself into a thorn bush, deliberately, as a punishment, a punishment for some sin I do not know of. Then, at the last moment, I am forced to admit to myself that I was right after all, and that it is really impossible to go down into the burrow without leaving the thing I love best, for a little while at least, at the mercy of all my enemies, on the ground, in the trees, in the air. And the danger is by no means a fanciful one, but very real. It need not be any particular enemy that is provoked to pursue me, it may very well be some chance innocent little creature, some disgusting little beast which follows me out of curiosity, and thus, without knowing it, becomes the leader of all the world against me; nor need it be even that, it may be – and that would be just as bad, indeed in some respects worse – it may be someone of my own kind, a connoisseur and prizer of burrows, a hermit, a lover of peace, but all the same a filthy scoundrel who wishes to be housed where he has not built. If he were actually to arrive now, if in his obscene lust he were to discover the entrance and set about working at it, lifting the moss; if he were actually to succeed, if he were actually to wriggle his way down in my stead, until only his hindquarters still showed; if all this were actually to happen, so that at last, casting all prudence to the winds, I might in my blind rage leap on him, maul him, tear the flesh from his bones, destroy him, drink his blood, and fling his corpse among the rest of my spoil, but above all – that is the main thing – were at last back in my burrow once more, I would have it in my heart to greet the labyrinth itself with rapture; yet first I would draw the moss covering over me, and I would want to rest, it seems to me, for all the remainder of my life. But nobody comes and I am left to my own resources. Perpetually obsessed by the sheer difficulty of the attempt, I lose much of my timidity, I no longer attempt even to appear to avoid the entrance, but make a hobby of prowling round it; by now it is almost as if I were the enemy spying out a suitable opportunity for successfully breaking in. If I only had someone I could trust to keep watch at my post of observation; then of course I could descend in perfect peace of mind. I should make an agreement with this trusty confederate of mine that he would keep a careful note of the state of things during my descent and for quite a long time afterwards, and if he saw any sign of danger knock on the moss covering, and if he saw nothing do nothing. With that a clean sweep would be made of all my fears, no residue would be left, or at most my confidant. For would he not demand some counterservice from

me; would he not at least want to see the burrow? That in itself, to let anyone freely into my burrow, would be exquisitely
painful to me. I built it for myself, not for visitors, and I think
I would refuse to admit him; not even though he alone made it
possible for me to get into the burrow would I let him in. But I
simply could not admit him, for either I must let him go in
first by himself, which is simply unimaginable, or we must both
descend at the same time, in which case the advantage I am
supposed to derive from him, that of being kept watch over,
would be lost. And what trust can I really put in him? Can I
trust one whom I have had under my eyes just as fully when I
can't see him, and the moss covering separates us? It is comparatively easy to trust anyone if you are supervising him or at
least can supervise him; perhaps it is possible even to trust someone at a distance; but completely to trust someone outside the
burrow when you are inside the burrow, that is in a different
world, that, it seems to me, is impossible. But such considerations are not in the least necessary; the mere reflection is
enough that during or after my descent one of the countless
accidents of existence might prevent my confidant from fulfill-
ing his duty, and what incalculable results might not the smallest accident of that kind have for me? No, if one takes it by and
large, I have no right to complain that I am alone and have
nobody that I can trust. I certainly lose nothing by that and
probably spare myself trouble. I can only trust myself and my
burrow. I should have thought of that before and taken measures to meet the difficulty that worries me so much now. When
I began the burrow it would at least have been partly possible.
I should have so constructed the first passage that it had two
entrances at a moderate distance from each other, so that after
descending through the one entrance with that slowness which
is unavoidable, I might rush at once through the passage to the
second entrance, slightly raise the moss covering, which would
be so arranged as to make that easy, and from there keep watch
on the position for several days and nights. That would have

been the only right way of doing it. True, the two entrances would double the risk, but that consideration need not delay me, for one of the entrances, serving merely as a post of observation, could be quite narrow. And with that I lose myself in a maze of technical speculations, I begin once more to dream my dream of a completely perfect burrow, and that somewhat calms me; with closed eyes I behold with delight perfect or almost perfect structural devices for enabling me to slip out and in unobserved. While I lie there thinking such things I admire these devices very greatly, but only as technical achievements, not as real advantages; for this freedom to slip out and in at will, what does it amount to? It is the mark of a restless nature, of inner uncertainty, disreputable desires, evil propensities that seem still worse when one thinks of the burrow, which is there at one's hand and can flood one with peace if one only remains quite open and receptive to it. For the present, however, I am outside it seeking some possibility of returning, and for that the necessary technical devices would be very desirable. But perhaps not so very desirable after all. Is it not a very grave injustice to the burrow to regard it in moments of nervous panic as a mere hole into which one can creep and be safe? Certainly it is a hole among other things, and a safe one, or should be, and when I picture myself in the midst of danger, then I insist with clenched teeth and all my will that the burrow should be nothing but a hole set apart to save me, and that it should fulfil that clearly defined function with the greatest possible efficiency, and I am ready to absolve it from every other duty. Now the truth of the matter – and one has no eye for that in times of great peril, and only by a great effort even in times when danger is threatening – is that in reality the burrow does provide a considerable degree of security, but by no means enough, for is one ever free from anxieties inside it? These anxieties are different from ordinary ones, prouder, richer in content, often long repressed, but in their destructive effects they are perhaps much the same as the anxieties that existence in the outer world gives rise to. Had I constructed the burrow exclusively to assure my safety I would not have been disappointed, it is true; nevertheless the relation between the enormous labour involved and the actual security it would provide, at least in so far as I could feel it and profit by it, would not have been in my favour. It is extremely painful to have to admit such things to oneself, but one is forced to do it, confronted by that entrance over there which now literally locks and bars itself against me, the builder and possessor. Yet the burrow is not a mere hole for taking refuge in. When I stand in the Castle Keep surrounded by my piled-up stores, surveying the ten passages which begin there, raised and sunken passages, vertical and rounded passages, wide and narrow passages, as the general plan dictates, and all alike still and empty, ready by their various routes to conduct me to all the other rooms, which are also still and empty – then all thought of mere safety is far from my mind, then I know that here is my castle, which I have wrested from the refractory soil with tooth and claw, with pounding and hammering blows, my castle which can never belong to anyone else, and is so essentially mine that I can calmly accept in it even my enemy's mortal stroke at the final hour, for my blood will ebb away here in my own soil and not be lost. And what but that is the meaning of the blissful hours which I pass, now peacefully slumbering, now happily keeping watch, in these passages, these passages which suit me so well, where one can stretch oneself out in comfort, roll about in childish delight, lie and dream, or sink into blissful sleep. And the smaller rooms, each familiar to me, so familiar that in spite of their complete similarity I can clearly distinguish one from the other with my eyes shut by the mere feel of the wall: they enclose me more peacefully and warmly than a bird is enclosed in its nest. And all, all still and empty.

But if that is the case, why do I hang back? Why do I dread the thought of the intruding enemy more than the possibility of never seeing my burrow again? Well, the latter alternative is fortunately an impossibility; there is no need for me even to take thought to know what the burrow means to me; I and the burrow belong so indissolubly together that in spite of all my fears I could make myself quite comfortable out here, and not even need to overcome my repugnance and open the door; I could be quite content to wait here passively, for nothing can part us for long, and somehow or other I shall quite certainly find myself in my burrow again. But on the other hand how much time may pass before then, and how many things may happen in that time, up here no less than down there? And it lies with me solely to curtail that interval and to do what is necessary at once.

And then, too exhausted to be any longer capable of thought, my head hanging, my legs trembling with fatigue, half-asleep, feeling my way rather than walking, I approach the entrance, slowly raise the moss covering, slowly descend, leaving the door open in my distraction for a needlessly long time, and presently remember my omission, and get out again to make it good – but what need was there to get out for that? All that was needed was to draw-to the moss covering; right; so I creep in again and now at last draw-to the moss covering. Only in this state, and in this state alone, can I achieve my descent. – So at last I lie down beneath the moss on the top of my blood-stained soil and can now enjoy my longed-for sleep. Nothing disturbs me, no one has tracked me down, above the moss everything seems to be quiet thus far at least, but even if all were not quiet I question whether I could stop to keep watch now; I have changed my place, I have left the upper world and am in my burrow, and I feel its effect at once. It is a new world, endowing me with new powers, and what I felt as fatigue up there is no longer that here. I have returned from a journey, dog-tired with my wanderings, but the sight of the old house, the thought of all the things that are waiting to be done, the necessity at least to cast a glance at all the rooms, but above all to make my way immediately to the Castle Keep; all this transforms my fatigue into ardent zeal; it is as though at the moment when I set foot in the burrow I had wakened from a long and profound sleep. My first task is a very laborious one and requires all my attention; I mean getting my soil through the narrow and thin-walled passages of the labyrinth. I shove with all my might, and the work gets done too, but far too slowly for me; to hasten it I drag part of my flesh supply back again and push my way over it and through it; now I have only a portion of my spoil before me and it is easier to make progress; but my road is so blocked by all this flesh in these narrow passages, through which it is not always easy for me to make my way when I am alone, that I could quite easily smother among my own stores; sometimes I can only rescue myself from their pressure by eating and drinking a clear space for myself. But the work of transport is successful, I finish it in quite a reasonable time, the labyrinth is behind me, I reach an ordinary passage and breathe freely, push my spoil through a communication passage into a main passage expressly designed for the purpose, a passage sloping down steeply to the Castle Keep. What is left to be done is not really work at all; my whole load rolls and flows down the passage almost of itself. The Castle Keep at last! At last I can dare to rest. Everything is unchanged, no great mishap seems to have occurred, the few little defects that I note at a first glance can soon be repaired; first, however, I must go my long round of all the passages, but that is no hardship, that is merely to commune again with friends, as I often did in the old days or – I am not so very old yet, but my memory of many things is already quite confused – as I often did, or as I have often imagined I did. I begin with the second passage, deliberately restraining myself, for once having seen the Castle Keep I have infinite time – within the burrow I always have infinite time – since everything I do there is valuable and important and satisfies me to a certain extent. I begin with the second passage, but break off in the middle and turn into the third passage and let it take me back again to the Castle Keep, and now of course I have to begin at the second passage once more, and so I play with my task and lengthen it out and smile to myself and congratulate myself and become quite dazed with all the work in front of me, but never think of turning aside from it. It is for your sake, ye passages and rooms, and you, Castle Keep, above all, that I have come back, counting my own life as nothing in the balance, after stupidly trembling for it for so long, and postponing my return to you. What do I care for danger now that I am with you? You belong to me, I to you, we are united; what can harm us? What if my foes should be assembling even now up above there and their muzzles be preparing to break through the moss? And with its silence and emptiness the burrow answers me, confirming my words. – But now a feeling of lassitude overcomes me and in some favourite room I curl myself up tentatively, I have not yet surveyed everything by a long way, though still resolved to examine everything to the very end; I have no intention of sleeping here, I have merely yielded to the temptation of making myself comfortable and pretending I want to sleep, I merely wish to find out if this is as good a place for sleeping in as it used to be. It is, but it is a better place for sleep than for wakening, and I remain lying where I am in deep slumber.

I must have slept for a long time. I was only wakened when I had reached the last light sleep which dissolves of itself, and it must have been very light, for it was an almost inaudible whistling noise that wakened me. I recognized what it was immediately; the smaller fry, whom I had allowed far too much latitude, had burrowed a new channel somewhere during my absence, this channel must have chanced to intersect an older one, the air was caught there, and that produced the whistling noise. What an indefatigably busy lot these smaller fry are, and what a nuisance their diligence can be! First I shall have to listen at the walls of my passages and locate the place of disturbance by experimental excavations, and only then will I be able to get rid of the noise. However, this new channel may be quite welcome as a further means of ventilation, if it can be fitted into the plan of the burrow. But after this I shall keep a much sharper eye on the small fry than I used to; I shall spare none of them.

As I have a good deal of experience in investigations of this kind the work probably will not take me long and I can start upon it at once; there are other jobs awaiting me, it is true, but this is the most urgent; I must have silence in my passages. This noise, however, is a comparatively innocent one; I did not hear it at all when I first arrived, although it must certainly have been there; I must first feel quite at home before I could hear it; it is, so to speak, audible only to the ear of the householder. And it is not even constant, as such noises usually are; there are long pauses, obviously caused by stoppages of the current of air. I start on my investigations, but I can't find the right place to begin at, and though I cut a few trenches I do it at random; naturally that has no effect, and the hard work of digging and the still harder work of filling the trenches up again and beating the earth firm is so much labour lost. I don't seem to be getting any nearer to the place where the noise is, it goes on always on the same thin note, with regular pauses, now a sort of whistling, but again like a kind of piping. Now I could leave it to itself for the time being; it is very disturbing, certainly, but there can hardly be any doubt that its origin is what I took it to be at first; so it can scarcely become louder, on the contrary such noises may quite well – though until now I have never had to wait so long for that to happen – may quite well vanish of themselves in the course of time through the continued labours of these little burrowers; and apart from that often chance itself puts one on the track of the disturbance, where systematic investigation has failed for a long time. In such ways I comfort myself, and resolve simply to continue my tour of the passages, and visit the rooms, many of which I have not even seen yet since my return, and enjoy myself contemplating the Castle Keep now and then between times; but my anxiety will not let me, and I must go on with my search. These little creatures take up much, far too much, time that could be better employed. In such cases as the present it is usually the technical problem that attracts me; for example, from the noise, which my ear can distinguish in all its finest shades, so that it has a perfectly clear outline to me, I deduce its cause, and now I am on fire to discover whether my conclusion is valid. And with good reason, for as long as that is not established I cannot feel safe, even if it were merely a matter of discovering where a grain of sand that had fallen from one of the walls had rolled to. And even a noise such as this is by no means a trifling matter, regarded from that angle. But whether trifling or important, I can find nothing, no matter how hard I search, or it may be that I find too much. This had to happen just in my favourite room, I think to myself, and I walk a fair good distance away from it, almost half-way along the passage leading to the next room; but I do this merely as a joke, pretending to myself that my favourite room is not alone to blame, but that there are disturbances elsewhere as well, and with a smile on my face I begin to listen; but soon I stop smiling, for, right enough, the same whistling meets me here, too. It is really nothing to worry about; sometimes I think that nobody but myself would hear it; it is true, I hear it now more and more distinctly, for my ear has grown keener through practice; though in reality it is exactly the same noise wherever I may hear it, as I have convinced myself by comparing my impressions. Nor is it growing louder; I recognize this when I listen in the middle of the passage instead of pressing my ear against the wall. Then it is only by straining my ears, indeed by lowering my head as well, that I can more guess at than hear the merest trace of a noise now and then. But it is this very uniformity of the noise everywhere that disturbs me most, for it cannot be made to agree with my original assumption. Had I rightly divined the cause of the noise, then it must have issued with greatest force from some given place, which it would be my task to discover, and after that have grown fainter and fainter. But if my hypothesis does not meet the case, what can the explanation be? There still remains the possibility that there are two noises, that up to now I have been listening at a good distance from the two centres, and that while its noise increases, when I draw near to one of them, the total result remains approximately the same for the ear in consequence of the lessening volume of sound from the other centre. Already I have almost fancied sometimes, when I have listened carefully, that I could distinguish, if very indistinctly, differences of tone which support this new assumption. In any case I must extend my sphere of investigation far farther than I have done. Accordingly I descend the passage to the Castle Keep and begin to listen there. Strange, the same noise there, too. Now it is a noise produced by the burrowing of some species of small fry who have infamously exploited my absence; in any case they have no intention of doing me harm, they are simply busied with their own work, and so long as no obstacle comes in their way they will keep on in the direction they have taken; I know all this, yet that they should have dared to approach the very Castle Keep itself is incomprehensible to me and fills me with agitation, and confuses the faculties which I need so urgently for the work before me. Here I have no wish to discover whether it is the unusual depth at which the Castle Keep lies, or its great extent and correspondingly powerful air suction, calculated to scare burrowing creatures away, or the mere fact that it is the Castle Keep, that by some channel or other has penetrated to their dull minds. In any case I have never noticed any sign of burrowing in the walls of the Castle Keep until now. Crowds of little beasts have come here, it is true, attracted by the powerful smells; here I have had a constant hunting-ground, but my quarry has always burrowed a way through in the upper passages, and come running down here, somewhat fearfully, but unable to withstand such a temptation. But now, it seems, they are burrowing in all the passages. If I had only carried out the best of the grand plans I thought out in my youth and early manhood, or rather, if I had only had the strength to carry them out, for there would have been no lack of will. One of these favourite plans of mine was to isolate the Castle Keep from its surroundings, that is to say, to restrict the thickness of its walls to about my own height, and leave a free space of about the same width all round the Castle Keep, except for a narrow foundation, which unfortunately would have to be left to bear up the whole. I had always pictured this free space, and not without reason, as the loveliest imaginable haunt. What a joy to lie pressed against the rounded outer wall, pull oneself up, let oneself slide down again, miss one's footing and find oneself on firm earth, and play all those games literally upon the Castle Keep and not inside it; to avoid the Castle Keep, to rest one's eyes from it whenever one wanted, to postpone the joy of seeing it until later and yet not have to do without it, but literally hold it safe between one's claws, a thing that is impossible if you have only an ordinary open entrance to it; but above all to be able to stand guard over it, and in that way to be so completely compensated for renouncing the actual sight of it that, if one had to choose between staying all one's life in the Castle Keep or in the free space outside it, one would choose the latter, content to wander up and down there all one's days and keep guard over the Castle Keep. Then there would be no noises in the walls, no insolent burrowing up to the very Keep itself; then peace would be assured there and I would be its guardian; then I would not have to listen with loathing to the burrowing of the small fry, but with delight to something that I cannot hear now at all: the murmurous silence of the Castle Keep.

But that beautiful dream is past and I must set to work, almost glad that now my work has a direct connexion with the Castle Keep, for that wings it. Certainly as I can see more and more clearly, I need all my energies for this task, which at first seemed quite a trifling one. I listen now at the walls of the Castle Keep, and wherever I listen, high or low, at the roof or the floor, at the entrance or in the corners, everywhere, everywhere, I hear the same noise. And how much time, how much care must be wasted in listening to that noise, with its regular pauses. One can, if one wishes, find a tiny deceitful comfort in the fact that here in the Castle Keep, because of its vastness, one hears nothing at all, as distinguished from the passages, when one stands back from the walls. Simply as a rest and a means to regain my composure I often make this experiment, listen intently and am overjoyed when I hear nothing. But the question still remains, what can have happened? Confronted with this phenomenon my original explanation completely falls to the ground. But I must also reject other explanations which present themselves to me. One could assume, for instance, that the noise I hear is simply that of the small fry themselves at their work. But all my experience contradicts this; I cannot suddenly begin to hear now a thing that I have never heard before though it was always there. My sensitiveness to disturbances in the burrow has perhaps become greater with the years, yet my hearing has by no means grown keener. It is of the very nature of small fry not to be heard. Would I have tolerated them otherwise? Even at the risk of starvation I would have exterminated them. But perhaps – this idea now insinuates itself – I am concerned here with some animal unknown to me. That is possible. True, I have observed the life down here long and carefully enough, but the world is full of diversity and is never wanting in painful surprises. Yet it cannot be a single animal, it must be a whole swarm that has suddenly fallen upon my domain, a huge swarm of little creatures, which as they are audible, must certainly be bigger than the small fry, but yet cannot be very much bigger, for the sound of their labours is itself very faint. It may be, then, a swarm of unknown creatures on their wanderings, who happen to be passing by my way, who disturb me, but will presently cease to do so. So I could really wait for them to pass, and need not put myself to the trouble of work that will be needless in the end. Yet if these creatures are strangers, why is it that I never see any of them? I have already dug a host of trenches, hoping to catch one of them, but I can find not a single one. Then it occurs to me that they may be quite tiny creatures, far tinier than any I am acquainted with, and that it is only the noise they make that is greater. Accordingly I investigate the soil I have dug up, I cast the lumps into the air so that they break into quite small particles, but the noise-makers are not among them. Slowly I come to realize that by digging such small fortuitous trenches I achieve nothing; in doing that I merely disfigure the walls of my burrow, scratching hastily here and there without taking time to fill up the holes again; at many places already there are heaps of earth which block my way and my view. Still, that is only a secondary worry; for now I can neither wander about my house, nor review it, nor rest; often already I have fallen asleep at my work in some hole or other, with one paw clutching the soil above me, from which in a semi-stupor I have been trying to tear a lump. I intend now to alter my methods. I shall dig a wide and carefully constructed trench in the direction of the noise and not cease from digging until, independent of all theories, I find the real cause of the noise. Then I shall eradicate it, if that is within my power, and if it is not, at least I shall know the truth. That truth will bring me either peace or despair, but whether the one or the other, it will be beyond doubt or question. This decision strengthens me. All that I have done till now seems to me far too hasty; in the excitement of my return, while I had not yet shaken myself free from the cares of the upper world, and was not yet completely penetrated by the peace of the burrow, but rather hypersensitive at having had to renounce it for such a long time, I was thrown into complete confusion of mind by an unfamiliar noise. And what was it? A faint whistling, audible only at long intervals, a mere nothing to which I don't say that one could actually get used, for no one could get used to it, but which one could, without actually doing anything about it at once, observe for a while, that is, listen every two hours, let us say, and patiently register the results, instead of, as I had done, keeping one's ear fixed to the wall and at every hint of noise tearing out a lump of earth, not really hoping to find anything, but simply so as to do something to give expression to one's inward agitation. All that will be changed now, I hope. And then, with furious shut eyes, I have to admit to myself that I hope nothing of the kind, for I am still trembling with agitation just as I was hours ago, and if my reason did not restrain me I would probably like nothing better than to start stubbornly and defiantly digging, simply for the sake of digging, at some place or other, whether I heard anything there or not; almost like the small fry, who burrow either without any object at all or simply because they eat the soil. My new and reasonable plan both tempts me and leaves me cold. There is nothing in it to object to, I at least know of no objection; it is bound, so far as I can see, to achieve my aim. And yet at bottom I do not believe in it; I believe in it so little that I do not even fear the terrors which its success may well bring. I do not believe even in a dreadful denouement; indeed it seems to me that I have been thinking ever since the first appearance of the noise of such a methodical trench, and have not begun upon it until now simply because I put no trust in it. In spite of that I shall of course start on the trench; I have no other alternative; but I shall not start at once, but postpone the task for a little while. If reason is to be reinstated on the throne again, it must be completely reinstated; I shall not rush blindly into my task. In any case I shall first repair the damage that I have done to the burrow with my wild digging; that will take a good long time, but it is necessary; if the new trench is really to reach its goal it will probably be long, and if it should lead to nothing at all it will be endless; in any case this task means a longish absence from the burrow, though an absence by no means so painful as an absence in the upper world, for I can interrupt my work whenever I like and pay a visit to my house; and even if I should not do that the air of the Castle Keep will be wafted to me and surround me while I work; nevertheless it means leaving the burrow and surrendering myself to an uncertain fate, and consequently I want to leave the burrow in good order behind me; it shall not be said that I, who am fighting for its peace, have myself destroyed that peace without reinstating it at once. So I begin by shovelling the soil back into the holes from which it was taken, a kind of work I am familiar with, that I have done countless times almost without regarding it as work, and at which, particularly as regards the final pressing and smoothing down – and this is no empty boast, but the simple truth – I am unbeatable. But this time everything seems difficult, I am too distracted, every now and then, in the middle of my work, I press my ear to the wall and listen, and without taking any notice let the soil that I have just lifted trickle back into the passage again. The final embellishments, which demand a stricter attention, I can hardly achieve at all. Hideous protuberances, disturbing cracks remain, not to speak of the fact that the old buoyancy simply cannot be restored again to a wall patched up in such a way. I try to comfort myself with the reflection that my present work is only temporary. When I return after peace has been restored I shall repair everything properly: work will be mere play to me then. Oh yes, work is mere play in fairy tales, and this comfort of mine belongs to the realm of fairy tales too. It would be far better to do the work thoroughly now, at once, far more reasonable than perpetually to interrupt it and wander off through the passages to discover new sources of noise, which is easy enough, all that is needed being to stop at any point one likes and listen. And that is not the end of my useless discoveries. Sometimes I fancy that the noise has stopped, for it makes long pauses; sometimes such a faint whistling escapes notice, one's own blood is pounding all too loudly in one's ears; then two pauses come one after another, and for a while one thinks that the whistling has stopped for ever. I listen no longer, I jump up, all life is transfigured; it is as if the fountains from which flows the silence of the burrow were unsealed. I refrain from verifying my discovery at once, I want first to find someone to whom in all good faith I can confide it, so I rush to the Castle Keep, I remember, for I and everything in me has awakened to new life, that I have eaten nothing for a long time, I snatch something or other from among my store of food half buried under debris and hurriedly begin to swallow it while I hurry back to the place where I made my incredible discovery, I only want to assure myself about it incidentally, perfunctorily, while I am eating; I listen, but the most perfunctory listening shows at once that I was shamefully deceived: away there in the distance the whistling still remains unshaken. And I spit out my food, and would like to trample it underfoot, and go back to my task, not caring which I take up; at any place where it seems to be needed, and there are enough places like that, I mechanically start on something or other, just as if the overseer had appeared and I must make a pretence of working for his benefit. But hardly have I begun in this fashion when it may happen that I make a new discovery. The noise seems to have become louder, not much louder, of course – here it is always a matter of the subtlest shades – but all the same sufficiently louder for the ear to recognize it clearly. And this growing-louder is like a coming-nearer; still more distinctly than you hear the increasing loud-ness of the noise you can literally see the step that brings it closer to you. You leap back from the wall, you try to grasp at once all the possible consequences that this discovery will bring with it. You feel as if you had never really organized the burrow for defence against attack; you had intended to do so, but despite all your experience of life the danger of an attack, and consequently the need to organize the place for defence, seemed remote – or rather not remote (how could it possibly be!) – but infinitely less important than the need to put it in a state where one could live peacefully; and so that consideration was given priority in everything relating to the burrow. Many things in this direction might have been done without affecting the plan

of the whole; most incomprehensibly they have been neglected.
I have had a great deal of luck all those years, luck has spoilt me;
I have had anxieties, but anxiety leads to nothing when you
have luck to back you.

The thing to do, really to do now, would be to go carefully
over the burrow and consider every possible means of defending it, work out a plan of defence and a corresponding plan of
construction, and then start on the work at once with the
vigour of youth. That is the work that would really be needed,
for which, I need not say, it is now far too late in the day; yet
that is what would really be needed, and not the digging of a
grand experimental trench, whose only real result would be to
deliver me hand and foot to the search for danger, out of the
foolish fear that it will not arrive quickly enough of itself.
Suddenly I cannot comprehend my former plan. I can find no
slightest trace of reason in what had seemed so reasonable;
once more I lay aside my work and even my listening; I have
no wish to discover any further signs that the noise is growing
louder; I have had enough of discoveries; I let everything slide;
I would be quite content if I could only still the conflict going
on within me. Once more I let my passages lead me where they
will, I come to more and more remote ones that I have not yet
seen since my return, and that are quite unsullied by my
scratching paws, and whose silence rises up to meet me and
sinks into me. I do not surrender to it, I hurry on, I do not
know what I want, probably simply to put off the hour. I stray
so far that I find myself at the labyrinth; the idea of listening
beneath the moss covering tempts me; such distant things,
distant for the moment, chain my interest. I push my way up
and listen. Deep stillness; how lovely it is here, outside there
nobody troubles about my burrow, everybody has his own
affairs, which have no connexion with me; how have I managed to achieve this state of things with all my calculations?
Here under the moss covering is perhaps the only place in my
burrow now where I can listen for hours and hear nothing. A

complete reversal of things in the burrow; what was once the place of danger has become a place of tranquillity, while the Castle Keep has been plunged into the bustle of the world and all its perils. Still worse, even here there is no peace in reality, here nothing has changed; silent or vociferous, danger lies in ambush as before above the moss, but I have grown insensitive to it, my mind is far too much taken up with the whistling in my walls. Is my mind really taken up with it? It grows louder, it comes nearer, but I wriggle my way through the labyrinth and make a couch for myself up here under the moss; it is almost as if I were already leaving the house to the whistler, content if I can only have a little peace up here. To the whistler? Have I come, then, to a new conclusion concerning the cause of the noise? But surely the noise is caused by the channels bored by the small fry? Is not that my considered opinion? It seems to me that I have not retreated from it thus far. And if the noise is not caused directly by these channels, it is indirectly. And even if it should have no connexion with them whatever, one is not at liberty to make a *priori* assumptions, but must wait until one finds the cause, or it reveals itself. One could play with hypotheses, of course, even at this stage; for instance it is possible that there has been a water burst at some distance away, and that what seems a piping or whistling to me is in reality a gurgling. But apart from the fact that I have no experience in that sphere – the groundwater that I found at the start I drained away at once, and in this sandy soil it has never returned – apart from this fact the noise is undeniably a whistling and simply not to be translated into a gurgling. But what avails all exhortations to be calm; my imagination will not rest, and I have actually come to believe – it is useless to deny it to myself – that the whistling is made by some beast, and moreover not by a great many small ones, but by a single great one. Many signs contradict this. The noise can be heard everywhere and always at the same strength, and moreover uniformly, both by day and night. At first, therefore, one cannot but incline to the hypothesis of a great number of little animals; but as I must have found some of them during my digging and I have found nothing, it only remains for me to assume the existence of a great beast, especially as the things that seem to contradict the hypothesis are merely things which make the beast, not so much impossible, as merely dangerous beyond all one's powers of conception. For that reason alone have I stuck out against this hypothesis. I shall cease from this self-deception. For a long time already I have played with the idea that the beast can be heard at such a great distance because it works so furiously; it burrows as fast through the ground as another animal can walk on the open road; the ground still trembles at its burrowing when it has ceased; this reverberation and the noise of the boring itself unite into one sound at such a great distance, and I, as I hear only the last dying ebb of that sound, hear it always at the same uniform strength. It follows from this also that the beast is not making for me, seeing that the noise never changes; more likely it has a plan in view whose purpose I cannot decipher; I merely assume that the beast – and I make no claim whatever that it knows of my existence – is encircling me; it has probably made several circles round my burrow already since I began to observe it. The nature of the noise, the piping or whistling, gives me much food for thought. When I scratch and scrape in the soil in my own fashion the sound is quite different. I can explain the whistling only in this way: that the beast's chief means of burrowing is not its claws, which it probably employs merely as a secondary resource, but its snout or its muzzle, which, of course, apart from its enormous strength, must also be fairly sharp at the point. It probably bores its snout into the earth with one mighty push and tears out a great lump; while it is doing that I hear nothing; that is the pause; but then it draws in the air for a new push. This indrawal of its breath, which must be an earth-shaking noise, not only because of the beast's strength, but of its haste, its furious lust for work as well: this noise I hear then as a faint whistling. But quite incomprehensible remains the beast's capacity to work without stopping; perhaps the short pauses provide also the opportunity of snatching a moment's rest; but apparently the beast has never yet allowed itself a really long rest, day and night it goes on burrowing, always with the same freshness and vigour, always thinking of its object, which must be achieved with the utmost expedition, and which it has the ability to achieve with ease. Now I could not have foreseen such an opponent. But apart altogether from the beast's peculiar characteristics, what is happening now is only something which I should really have feared all the time, something against which I should have been constantly prepared: the fact that someone would come. By what chance can everything have flowed on so quietly and happily for such a long time? Who can have diverted my enemies from their path, and forced them to make a wide detour round my property? Why have I been spared for so long, only to be delivered to such terrors now? Compared with this, what are all the petty dangers in brooding over which I have spent my life! As owner of the burrow I had hoped to be in a stronger position than any enemy who might chance to appear. But simply by virtue of being owner of this great vulnerable edifice I am obviously defenceless against any serious attack. The joy of possessing it has spoilt me, the vulnerability of the burrow has made me vulnerable; any wound to it hurts me as if I myself were hit. It is precisely this that I should have foreseen; instead of thinking only of my own defence – and how perfunctorily and vainly I have done even that – I should have thought of the defence of the burrow. Above all, provision should have been made for cutting off sections of the burrow, and as many as possible of them, from the endangered sections when they are attacked; this should have been done by means of improvised land-slides, calculated to operate at a moment's notice; moreover these should have been so thick, and have provided such an effectual barrier, that the attacker would not even guess that the real burrow only began at the other side. More, these land-slides should have been so devised that they not only concealed the burrow, but also entombed the attacker. Not the slightest attempt have I made to carry out such a plan, nothing at all has been done in this direction, I have been as thoughtless as a child, I have passed my manhood's years in childish games, I have done nothing but play even with the thought of danger, I have shirked really taking thought for actual danger. And there has been no lack of warning.

Nothing, of course, approaching the present situation has happened before; nevertheless there was an incident not unlike it when the burrow was only beginning. The main difference between that time and this is simply that the burrow was only beginning then. ... In those days I was literally nothing more than a humble apprentice in his first year, the labyrinth was only sketched out in rough outline, I had already dug a little room, but the proportions and the execution of the walls were sadly bungled; in short everything was so tentative that it could only be regarded as an experiment, as something which, if one lost patience some day, one could leave lying as it was without much regret. Then one day as I lay on a heap of earth resting from my labours – I have rested far too often from my labours all my life – suddenly I heard a noise in the distance. Being young at the time, I was less frightened than curious. I left my work to look after itself and set myself to listen; I listened and listened, and had no wish to fly up to my moss covering and stretch myself out there so that I might not hear. I did listen, at least. I could clearly recognize that the noise came from some kind of burrowing similar to my own; it was somewhat fainter, of course, but how much of that might be put down to the distance one could not tell. I was intensely interested, but otherwise calm and cool. Perhaps I am in somebody's else's burrow, I thought to myself, and now the owner is boring his way towards me. If that assumption had proved to be correct I would have gone away, for I have never had any desire for conquest or bloodshed, and begun building somewhere else. But after all I was still young and still without a burrow, so I could remain quite cool. Besides, the further course of the noise brought no real cause for apprehension, except that it was not easy to explain. If whoever was boring there was really making for me, because he had heard me boring, then if he changed his direction, as now actually happened, it could not be told whether he did this because my pause for rest had deprived him of any definite point to make towards, or because – which was more plausible – he had himself changed his plans. But perhaps I had been deceived altogether, and he had never been actually making in my direction; at any rate the noise grew louder for a while as if he were drawing nearer, and being young at that time I probably would not have been displeased to see the burrower suddenly rising from the ground; but nothing of that kind happened, at a certain point the sound of boring began to weaken, it grew fainter and fainter, as if the burrower were gradually diverging from his first route, and suddenly it broke off altogether, as if he had decided now to take the diametrically opposite direction and were making straight away from me into the distance. For a long time I still went on listening for him in the silence, before I returned once more to my work. Now that warning was definite enough, but I soon forgot it, and it scarcely influenced my building plans.

Between that day and this lie my years of maturity, but is it not as if there were no interval at all between them? I still take long rests from my labours and listen at the wall, and the burrower has changed his intention anew, he has turned back, he is returning from his journey, thinking he has given me ample time in the interval to prepare for his reception. But on my side everything is worse prepared for than it was then; the great burrow stands defenceless, and I am no longer a young apprentice, but an old architect, and the powers I still have fail me when the decisive hour comes; yet old as I am it seems to me that I would gladly be still older, so old that I should never be able to rise again from my resting-place under the moss. For to be honest I cannot endure the place, I rise up and rush, as if I had filled myself up there with new anxieties instead of peace, down into the house again. What was the state of things the last time I was here? Had the whistling grown fainter? No, it had grown louder. I listen at ten places chosen at random and definitely note my own disappointment; the whistling is just the same as ever, nothing has altered. Up there under the moss no change touches one, there one is at peace, uplifted above time; but here every instant frets and gnaws at the listener. I go once more the long road to the Castle Keep, all my surroundings seem filled with agitation, seem to be looking at me, and then look away again so as not to annoy me, yet cannot refrain the very next moment from trying to read the saving solution from my expression. I shake my head, I have not yet found any solution. Nor do I go to the Castle Keep in pursuance of any plan. I pass the spot where I had intended to begin the experimental trench, I look it over once more, it would have been an admirable place to begin at, the trench's course would have been in the direction where lay the majority of the tiny ventilation holes, which would have greatly lightened my labours; perhaps I should not have had to dig very far, should not even have had to dig to the source of the noise; perhaps if I had listened at the ventilation holes it would have been enough. But no consideration is potent enough to animate me to this labour of digging. This trench will bring me certainty, you say? I have reached the stage where I no longer wish to have certainty. In the Castle Keep I choose a lovely piece of flayed red flesh and creep with it into one of the heaps of earth; there I shall have silence at least, such silence, at any rate, as still can be said to exist here. I munch and nibble at the flesh, think of the strange beast going its own road in the distance, and then again that I should enjoy my store of food as fully as possible, while I still have the chance. This last is probably the sole plan I have left that I can carry out. For the rest I try to unriddle the beast's plans. Is it on its wanderings, or is it working on its own burrow? If it is on its wanderings then perhaps an understanding with it might be possible. If it should really break through to the burrow I shall give it some of my store and it will go on its way again. It will go its way again, a fine story. Lying on my heap of earth I can naturally dream of all sorts of things, even of an understanding with the beast, though I know well enough that no such thing can happen, and that at the instant when we see each other, more, at the moment when we merely guess at each other's presence, we shall both blindly bare our claws and teeth, neither of us a second before or after the other, both of us filled with a new and different hunger, even if we should already be gorged to bursting. And with entire justice, for who, even if he were merely on his wanderings, would not change his itinerary and his plans for the future on catching sight of the burrow? But perhaps the beast is digging in its own burrow, in which case I cannot even dream of an understanding. Even if it should be such a peculiar beast as to be able to tolerate a neighbour near its burrow, it could not tolerate my burrow, it would not tolerate in any case a neighbour who could be clearly heard. Now actually the beast seems to be a great distance away: if it would only withdraw a little farther the noise, too, would probably disappear; perhaps in that case everything would be peaceful again as in the old days; all this would then become a painful but salutary lesson, spurring me on to make the most diverse improvements on the burrow; if I have peace, and danger does not immediately threaten me, I am still quite fit for all sorts of hard work; perhaps, considering the enormous possibilities which its powers of work open before it, the beast has given up the idea of extending its burrow in my direction, and is compensating itself for that in some other one. That consummation also cannot, of course, be brought about by negotiation but only by the beast itself, or by some compulsion exercised from my side. In both cases the decisive factor will be whether the beast knows about me, and if so what it knows. The more I reflect upon it the more improbable does it seem to me that the beast has even heard of me; it is possible, though unimaginable, that it can have received news of me through some other channel, but it has certainly never heard me. So long as I still knew nothing about it, it simply cannot have heard me, for at that time I kept very quiet, nothing could be more quiet than my return to the burrow; afterwards, when I dug the experimental trenches, perhaps it could have heard me, though my style of digging makes very little noise; but if it had heard me I must have noticed some sign of it, the beast must at least have stopped its work every now and then to listen. But all remained unchanged.

In the Penal Settlement

'IT's a remarkable piece of apparatus,' said the officer to the explorer and surveyed with a certain air of admiration the apparatus which was after all quite familiar to him. The explorer seemed to have accepted merely out of politeness the Commandant's invitation to witness the execution of a soldier condemned to death for disobedience and insulting behaviour to a superior. Nor did the colony itself betray much interest in this execution. At least, in the small sandy valley, a deep hollow surrounded on all sides by naked crags, there was no one present save the officer, the explorer, the condemned man, who was a stupid-looking wide-mouthed creature with bewildered hair and face, and the soldier who held the heavy chain controlling the small chains locked on the prisoner's ankles, wrists, and neck, chains which were themselves attached to each other by communicating links. In any case, the condemned man looked so like a submissive dog that one might have thought he could be left to run free on the surrounding hills and would only need to be whistled for when the execution was due to begin.

The explorer did not much care about the apparatus and walked up and down behind the prisoner with almost visible indifference, while the officer made the last adjustments, now creeping beneath the structure, which was bedded deep in the earth, now climbing a ladder to inspect its upper parts. These were tasks that might well have been left to a mechanic, but the officer performed them with great zeal, whether because he was a devoted admirer of the apparatus or because for other reasons the work could be entrusted to no one else. 'Ready now!' he called at last and climbed down from the ladder. He looked uncommonly limp, breathed with his mouth wide open and had tucked two fine ladies' handkerchiefs under the collar of his uniform. 'These uniforms are too heavy for the tropics, surely,' said the explorer, instead of making some inquiry about the apparatus, as the officer had expected. 'Of course,' said the officer, washing his oily and greasy hands in a bucket of water that stood ready, 'but they mean home to us; we don't want to forget about home. Now just have a look at this machine,' he added at once, simultaneously drying his hands on a towel and indicating the apparatus. 'Up till now everything has to be set by hand, but from this moment it works all by itself.' The explorer nodded and followed him. The officer, anxious to secure himself against all contingencies, said: 'Things sometimes go wrong, of course; I hope that nothing goes wrong today, but we have to allow for the possibility. The machinery should go on working continuously for twelve hours. But if anything does go wrong it will only be some small matter, and can be set right at once.'

'Won't you take a seat?' he asked finally, drawing a cane chair out from among a heap of them and offering it to the explorer, who could not refuse it. He was now sitting at the edge of a grave, into which he glanced for a fleeting moment. It was not very deep. On one side of the grave the excavated soil had been piled up in a rampart, on the other side of it stood the apparatus.

'I don't know,' said the officer, 'if the Commandant has already explained this apparatus to you.' The explorer waved one hand vaguely; the officer asked for nothing better, since now he could explain the apparatus himself. 'This apparatus,' he said, taking hold of a crank-handle and leaning against it, 'was invented by our former Commandant. I assisted at the very earliest experiments and had a share in all the work until its completion. But the credit of inventing it belongs to him alone. Have you ever heard of our former Commandant? No? Well, it isn't saying too much if I tell you that the organization of the whole penal settlement is his work. We who were his friends knew even before he died that the organization of the colony was so perfect that his successor, even with a thousand new schemes in his head, would find it impossible to alter any-thing, at least for many years to come. And our prophecy has come true; the new Commandant has had to acknowledge its truth. A pity you never met the old Commandant! But,' the officer interrupted himself, 'I am rambling on, and here stands his apparatus before us. It consists, as you see, of three parts. In the course of time each of these parts has acquired a kind of popular nickname. The lower one is called the "Bed", the upper one the "Designer", and this one here in the middle that moves up and down is called the "Harrow".' 'The Harrow?' asked the explorer. He had not been listening very attentively, the glare of the sun in the shadeless valley was altogether too strong, it was difficult to collect one's thoughts. All the more did he ad-mire the officer, who in spite of his tight-fitting full-dress uni-form coat, amply befrogged and weighed down by epaulettes, was pursuing his subject with such enthusiasm and, besides talking, was still tightening a screw here and there with a span-ner. As for the soldier, he seemed to be in much the same condi-tion as the explorer. He had wound the prisoner's chain round both his wrists, propped himself on his rifle, let his head hang and was paying no attention to anything. That did not sur-prise the explorer, for the officer was speaking French, and cer-tainly neither the soldier nor the prisoner understood a word of French. It was all the more remarkable, therefore, that the prisoner was none the less making an effort to follow the officer's explanations. With a kind of drowsy persistence he directed his gaze wherever the officer pointed a finger, and at the interruption of the explorer's question he, too, as well as the officer, looked round.

'Yes, the Harrow,' said the officer, 'a good name for it. The needles are set in like the teeth of a harrow and the whole thing works something like a harrow, although its action is limited to one place and contrived with much more artistic skill. Anyhow, you'll soon understand it. On the Bed here the condemned man is laid – I'm going to describe the apparatus first before I set it in motion. Then you'll be able to follow the proceedings better. Besides, one of the cog-wheels in the Designer is badly worn; it creaks a lot when it's working; you can hardly hear yourself speak; spare parts, unfortunately, are difficult to get here. Well, here is the Bed, as I told you. It is completely covered with a layer of cotton-wool; you'll find out why later. On this cotton-wool the condemned man is laid, face down, quite naked, of course; here are straps for the hands, here for the feet, and here for the neck, to bind him fast. Here at the head of the Bed, where the man, as I said, first lays down his face, is this little gag of felt, which can be easily regulated to go straight into his mouth. It is meant to keep him from screaming and biting his tongue. Of course the man is forced to take the felt into his mouth, for otherwise his neck would be broken by the strap.' 'Is that cotton-wool?' asked the explorer, bending forward. 'Yes, certainly,' said the officer, with a smile, 'feel it for yourself.' He took the explorer's hand and guided it over the Bed. 'It's specially prepared cotton-wool, that's why it looks so different; I'll tell you presently what it's for.' The explorer already felt a dawning interest in the apparatus; he sheltered his eyes from the sun with one hand and gazed up at the structure. It was a huge affair. The Bed and the Designer were of the same size and looked like two dark wooden chests. The Designer hung about two metres above the Bed; each of them was fastened at the corners by four rods of brass that almost flashed out rays in the sunlight. Beneath the chests shuttled the Harrow on a ribbon of steel.

The officer had scarcely noticed the explorer's previous indifference, but he was now well aware of his dawning interest; so he stopped explaining in order to leave a space of time for quiet observation. The condemned man imitated the explorer; since he could not use a hand to shelter his eyes he gazed upwards without shade.

'Well, the man lies down,' said the explorer, leaning back in his chair and crossing his legs.

'Yes,' said the officer, pushing his cap back a little and passing one hand over his heated face, 'now listen! Both the Bed and the Designer have an electric battery each; the Bed needs one for itself, the Designer one for the Harrow. As soon as the man is strapped down, the Bed is set in motion. It quivers in minute, very rapid vibrations, both from side to side and up and down. You will have seen similar apparatus in hospitals; but in our Bed the movements are all precisely calculated; you see, they have to correspond very exactly to the movements of the Harrow. And the Harrow is the instrument for the actual execution of the sentence.'

'And how does the sentence run?' asked the explorer.

'You don't know that either?' said the officer in amazement, and bit his lips. 'Forgive me if my explanations seem rather incoherent. I do beg your pardon. You see, the Commandant always used to do the explaining; but the new Commandant shirks this duty; yet that such an important visitor' – the explorer tried to deprecate the honour with both hands, the officer, however, insisted – 'that such an important visitor should not even be told about the kind of sentence we pass is a new development, which –' he was just on the point of using strong language but checked himself and said only: 'I was not informed, it is not my fault. In any case, I am certainly the best person to explain our procedure, since I have in here' – he patted his breast-pocket – 'the relevant drawings made by our former Commandant.'

'The Commandant's own drawings?' asked the explorer. 'Did he combine everything in himself, then? Was he soldier, judge, mechanic, chemist, and draughtsman?'

'Indeed he was,' said the officer, nodding assent, with a remote, glassy look. Then he inspected his hands critically; they did not seem clean enough to him for touching the drawings; so he went over to the bucket and washed them again. Then he drew out a small leather brief-case and said: 'Our sentence does not sound severe. Whatever commandment the condemned man has disobeyed is written upon his body by the Harrow. This condemned man, for instance,' – the officer indicated the man – 'will have written on his body: HONOUR THY SUPER-IORS!'

The explorer glanced at the man; he stood, as the officer pointed him out, with bent head, apparently listening with all his ears in an effort to catch what was being said. Yet the movement of his blubber lips, closely pressed together, showed clearly that he could not understand a word. Many questions were troubling the explorer, but at the sight of the condemned man he asked only: 'Does he know his sentence?' 'No – ' said the officer, eager to go on with his exposition, but the explorer interrupted him: 'He doesn't know the sentence that has been passed on him?' 'No – ' said the officer again, pausing a moment as if to let the explorer elaborate his question, and then said: 'There would be no point in telling him. He'll learn it corporally, on his person ' The explorer intended to make no answer, but he felt the prisoner's gaze turned on him; it seemed to ask if he approved such goings on. So he bent forward again, having already leaned back in his chair, and put another question: 'But surely he knows that he has been sentenced?' 'Nor that either,' said the officer, smiling at the explorer, as if expecting him to make further surprising remarks. 'No,' said the explorer, wiping his forehead, 'then he cannot know either whether his defence was effective?' 'He has had no chance of putting up a defence,' said the officer, turning his eyes away, as if speaking to himself and so sparing the explorer the shame of hearing self-evident matters explained. 'But he must have had some chance of defending himself,' said the explorer, and rose from his seat.

The officer understood that he was in danger of having his exposition of the apparatus held up for a long time; so he went up to the explorer, took him by the arm, waved a hand towards the condemned man, who was standing very straight now that he had so obviously become the centre of attention – the soldier had also given the chain a jerk – and said: 'This is how the matter stands. I have been appointed judge in this penal settlement; despite my youth; for I was the former Commandant's assistant in all penal matters and know more about the apparatus than anyone. My guiding principle is this: Guilt is never to be doubted. Other courts cannot follow that principle, for they consist of several opinions and have higher courts to scrutinize them. That is not the case here, or at least, it was not the case in the former Commandant's time. The new man has certainly shown some inclination to interfere with my judgements, but so far I have succeeded in fending him off and will go on succeeding. You will like to have the case explained; it is quite simple, like all of them. A captain reported to me this morning that this man, who had been assigned to him as a servant and slept before his door, had been asleep on duty. It is his duty, you see, to get up every time the hour strikes and salute the captain's door. Not an exacting duty, and very necessary, since he has to be a sentry as well as a servant, and must be alert in both functions. Last night the captain wanted to see if the man was doing his duty. He opened the door as the clock struck two and there was his man curled up asleep. He took a riding-whip and lashed him across the face. Instead of getting up and begging pardon, the man caught hold of his master's legs, shook him and cried: "Throw that whip away or I'll eat you alive." That's the evidence. The captain came to me an hour ago, I wrote down his statement and appended the sentence to it. Then I had the man put in chains. That was all quite simple. If I had first called the man before me and interrogated him, things would have got into a confused tangle. He would have told lies, and had I exposed these lies he would have backed them up with more lies, and so on and so forth. As it is, I've got him and I won't let him go. Is that quite clear now? But we're wasting time, the execution should be beginning and I haven't finished explaining the apparatus yet.' He pressed the explorer back into his chair, went up again to the apparatus and began: 'As you see, the shape of the Harrow corresponds to the human form; here is the harrow for the torso, here are the harrows for the legs. For the head there is only this one small spike. Is that quite clear?' He bent amiably forward towards the explorer, eager to provide the most comprehensive explanations.

The explorer considered the Harrow with a frown. Such a version of judicial procedure displeased him. He had to remind himself that this was in any case a penal settlement where extraordinary measures were needed and that military discipline must be enforced to the last. Yet he felt that some hope might be set on the new Commandant, who was apparently of a mind to bring in, although gradually, a new kind of procedure which the officer's narrow mind was incapable of understanding. This train of thought prompted his next question: 'Will the Commandant attend the execution?' 'It is not certain,' said the officer, wincing at the direct question, and his friendly expression darkened. 'That is just why we have to lose no time. Much as I dislike it, I shall have to cut my explanations short. But, of course, tomorrow, when the apparatus has been cleaned – its one drawback is that it gets so messy – I can recapitulate all the details. For the present, then, only the essentials. – When the man lies down on the Bed and it begins to vibrate, the Harrow is lowered on to his body. It regulates itself automatically so that the needles barely touch his skin; once contact is made the steel ribbon stiffens immediately into a rigid band. And then the performance begins. An ignorant onlooker would see no difference between one punishment and another. The Harrow appears to do its work with uniform regularity. As it quivers, its points pierce the skin of the body which is itself quivering from the vibration of the Bed. So that the actual progress of the sentence can be watched, the Harrow is made of glass. Getting the needles fixed in the glass was a technical problem, but after many experiments we overcame the difficulty. No trouble was too great for us to take, you see. And now anyone can look through the glass and watch the inscription taking form on the body. Wouldn't you care to come a little nearer and have a look at the needles?'

The explorer got up slowly, walked across and bent over the Harrow. 'You see,' said the officer, 'there are two kinds of needles arranged in multiple patterns. Each long needle has a short one beside it. The long needle does the writing, and the short needle sprays a jet of water to wash away the blood and keep the inscription clear. Blood and water together are then conducted here through small runnels into this main runnel and down a waste-pipe into the grave.' With his finger the officer traced the exact course taken by the blood and water. To make the picture as vivid as possible he held both hands below the outlet of the waste-pipe as if to catch the outflow, and when he did this the explorer drew back his head and, feeling behind him with one hand, sought to return to his chair. To his horror he found that the condemned man too had obeyed the officer's invitation to examine the Harrow at close quarters and had followed him. He had pulled forward the sleepy soldier with the chain and was bending over the glass. One could see that his uncertain eyes were trying to perceive what the two gentlemen had been looking at, but, since he had not understood the explanation, he could not make head or tail of it. He was peering this way and that way. He kept running his eyes along the glass. The explorer wanted to drive him away, since what he was doing was probably culpable. But the officer firmly restrained the explorer with one hand and with the other took a clod of earth from the rampart and threw it at the soldier. He opened his eyes with a jerk, saw what the condemned man had dared to do, let his rifle fall, dug his heels into the ground, dragged his prisoner back so that he stumbled and fell immediately, and then stood looking down at him, watching him struggling and rattling in his chains. 'Set him on his feet!' yelled the officer, for he noticed that the explorer's attention was being too much distracted by the condemned man. In fact the explorer was even leaning right across the Harrow, without taking any notice of it, intent only in finding out what was happening to the condemned man. 'Be careful with him!' cried the officer again. He ran round the apparatus, himself caught the condemned man under the shoulders and with the soldier's help got him up on his feet, which kept slithering from under him.

'Now I know all about it,' said the explorer, as the officer came back to him. 'All except the most important thing,' the latter said, seizing the explorer's arm and pointing upwards: 'In the Designer are all the cog-wheels that control the movements of the Harrow, and this machinery is regulated according to the inscription demanded by the sentence. I am still using the guiding plans drawn by the former Commandant. Here they are' – he extracted some sheets from the leather brief-case – 'but I'm sorry I can't let you handle them, they are my most precious possessions. Just take a seat and I'll hold them in front of you like this, then you'll be able to see everything quite well.' He spread out the first sheet of paper. The explorer would have liked to say something appreciative, but all he could see was a labyrinth of lines crossing and re-crossing each other, which covered the paper so thickly that it was difficult to discern the blank spaces between them. 'Read it,' said the officer. 'I can't,' said the explorer. 'Yet it's clear enough,' said the officer. 'It's very ingenious,' said the explorer evasively, 'but I can't make it out.' 'Yes,' said the officer with a laugh, putting the paper away again, 'it's no calligraphy for school children. It needs to be studied closely. I'm quite sure that in the end you would understand it too. Of course the script can't be a simple one; it's not supposed to kill a man straight off, but only after an interval of, on an average, twelve hours; the turning-point is reckoned to come at the sixth hour. So there have to be lots and lots of flourishes around the actual script; the script itself runs round the body only in a narrow girdle; the rest of the body is reserved for the embellishments. Can you appreciate now the work accomplished by the Harrow and the whole apparatus? Just watch it!' He ran up the ladder, turned a wheel, called down: 'Look out, keep to one side!' and everything started working. If the wheel had not creaked, it would have been marvellous. The officer, as if surprised by the noise of the wheel, shook his fist at it, then spread out his arms in excuse to the explorer and climbed down rapidly to peer at the working of the machine from below. Something perceptible to no one save himself was still not in order; he clambered up again, groped about with both hands in the interior of the Designer, then slid down one of the rods, instead of using the ladder, so as to get down quicker, and with the full force of his lungs, to make himself heard at all in the noise, yelled in the explorer's ear: 'Can you follow it? The Harrow is beginning to write; when it finishes the first draft of the inscription on the back, the layer of cotton-wool begins to roll and slowly turns the body over, to give the Harrow fresh space for writing. Meanwhile the raw part that has been written on lies on the cotton-wool, which is specially prepared to staunch the bleeding and so makes all ready for a new deepening of the script. Then these teeth at the edge of the Harrow, as the body turns farther round, tear the cotton-wool away from the wounds, throw it into the grave and there is more work for the Harrow. So it keeps on writing deeper and deeper for the whole twelve hours. The first six hours the condemned man stays alive almost as before, he suffers only pain. After two hours the felt gag is taken away, for he has no longer strength to scream. Here, into this electrically heated basin at the head of the Bed, some warm rice-pap is poured, from which the man, if he feels like it, can take as much as his tongue can lap. Not one of them ever misses the chance. I can remember none, and my experience is extensive. Only about the sixth hour does the man lose all desire to eat. I usually kneel down here at that moment and observe this phenomenon. The man rarely swallows his last mouthful, he only rolls it round his mouth and spits it out into the grave. I have to duck just then or he would spit it in my face. But how quiet he grows at just about the sixth hour! Enlightenment comes to the most dull-witted. It begins around the eyes. From there it radiates. A moment that might tempt one to get under the Harrow with him. Nothing more happens after that, the man only begins to understand the inscription, he purses his mouth as if he were listening. You have seen how difficult it is to decipher the script with one's eyes; but our man deciphers it with his wounds. To be sure, that is a hard task; he needs six hours to accomplish it. By that time the Harrow has pierced him quite through and casts him into the grave, where he pitches down upon the blood and water and the cotton-wool. Then the judgement has been fulfilled, and we, the soldier and I, bury him.'

The explorer had inclined his ear to the officer and, with his hands in his jacket pockets, watched the machine at work. The condemned man watched it too, but uncomprehendingly. He bent forward a little and was intent on the moving needles, when the soldier, at a sign from the officer, slashed through his shirt and trousers from behind with a knife, so that they fell off; he tried to catch at his falling clothes to cover his nakedness, but the soldier lifted him into the air and shook the last remnants from him. The officer stopped the machine, and in the sudden silence the condemned man was laid under the Harrow. The chains were loosened and the straps fastened on instead; in the first moment that seemed almost a relief to the condemned man. And now the Harrow was adjusted a little lower, since he was a thin man. When the needle-points touched him a shudder ran over his skin; while the soldier was busy strapping his right hand, he flung out his left hand blindly; but it happened to be in the direction towards where the explorer was standing. The officer kept watching the explorer sideways, as if seeking to read from his face the impression made on him by the execution, which had been at least cursorily explained to him.

The wrist-strap broke; probably the soldier had drawn it too tight. The officer had to intervene, the soldier held up the broken piece of the strap to show him. So the officer went over to him and said, his face still turned towards the explorer: 'This is a very complex machine, things are always breaking or giving way here and there; but one must not thereby allow oneself to be diverted in one's general judgement. In any case, this strap is easily made good; I shall simply use a chain; the delicacy of the vibrations for the right arm will, of course, be a little impaired.' And while he fastened the chain, he added: 'The resources for maintaining the machine are now very much reduced. Under the former Commandant I had free access to a sum of money set aside entirely for this purpose. There was a store, too, in which spare parts were kept for repairs of all kinds. I confess I have been almost prodigal with them, I mean in the past, not now as the new Commandant pretends, always looking for an excuse to attack our old way of doing things. Now he has taken charge of the machine money himself, and if I send for a new strap they ask for the broken old strap as evidence, and the new strap takes ten days to appear and then is of shoddy material and not much good. But how I am supposed to work the machine without a strap, that's something nobody bothers about.'

The explorer thought to himself: It's always a ticklish matter to intervene decisively in other people's affairs. He was neither a member of the penal colony nor a citizen of the state to which it belonged. Were he to denounce this execution or actually try to stop it, they could say to him: 'You are a stranger, mind your own business.' He could make no answer to that, unless he were to add that he was amazed at himself in this connexion, for he travelled only as an observer, with no intention at all of altering other people's methods of administering justice. Yet here he found himself strongly tempted. The injustice of the procedure and the inhumanity of the execution were undeniable. No one could suppose that he had any selfish interest in the matter, for the condemned man was a complete stranger, not a fellow countryman or even at all sympathetic to him. The explorer himself had recommendations from high quarters, had been received here with great courtesy, and the very fact that he had been invited to attend the execution seemed to suggest that his views would be welcome. And this was all the more likely since the Commandant, as he had heard only too plainly, was no upholder of the procedure and maintained an attitude almost of hostility to the officer.

At that moment the explorer heard the officer cry out in rage. He had just, with considerable difficulty, forced the felt gag into the condemned man's mouth when the man, in an irresistible access of nausea, shut his eyes and vomited. Hastily the officer snatched him away from the gag and tried to hold his head over the grave; but it was too late, the vomit was running all over the machine. 'It's all the fault of that Commandant!' cried the officer, senselessly shaking the brass rods in front, 'the machine is befouled like a pig-sty.' With trembling hands he indicated to the explorer what had happened. 'Have I not tried for hours at a time to get the Commandant to understand that the prisoner must fast for a whole day before the execution. But our new, mild doctrine thinks otherwise. The Commandant's ladies stuff the man's mouth with sugar-candy before he's led off. He has lived on stinking fish his whole life long and now he has to guzzle sugar-candy! But it could still be possible, I should have nothing to say against it, but why won't they get me a new felt gag, which I have been begging for the last three months. How should a man not feel sick when he takes a felt gag into his mouth which more than a hundred men have already slobbered and gnawed in their dying moments?'

The condemned man had laid his head down and looked peaceful, the soldier was busy trying to clean the machine with the condemned man's shirt. The officer advanced towards the explorer, who in some vague presentiment fell back a pace, but the officer seized him by the hand, and drew him to one side.

'I should like to exchange a few words with you in confidence,' he said. 'May I?' 'Of course,' said the explorer, and listened with downcast eyes.

'This procedure and method of execution, which you are now having the opportunity to admire, has at the moment no longer any open adherents in our colony. I am its sole advocate, and at the same time the sole advocate of the old Commandant's tradition. I can no longer reckon on any further extension of the method, it takes all my energy to maintain it as it is. During the old Commandant's lifetime the colony was full of his adherents; his strength of conviction I still have in some measure, but not an atom of his power; consequently the adherents have skulked out of sight, there are still many of them but none of them will admit it. If you were to go into the tea-house today, an execution day, and listen to what is being said, you would perhaps hear only ambiguous remarks. These would all be made by adherents, but under the present Commandant and his present doctrines they are of no use to me. And now I ask you: because of this Commandant and the women who influence him, is such a piece of work, the work of a life-time,' – he pointed to the machine – 'to fall into disuse? Ought one to let that happen? Even if one has only come as a stranger to our island for a few days? And yet there's no time to lose, an attack of some kind is impending on my function as a judge: conferences are already being held in the Commandant's office from which I am excluded; even your coming here today seems to me a significant move; they are cowards and use you as a screen, you, a stranger. How different an execution was in the old days! A whole day before the ceremony the valley was packed with people; they all came only to look on; early in the morning the Commandant appeared with his ladies; fanfares roused the whole camp; I reported that everything was in readiness; the assembled company – no high official dared to absent himself – arranged itself round the machine; this pile of cane chairs is a miserable survival from that epoch. The machine was freshly cleaned and glittering, I got new spare parts for almost every execution. Before hundreds of spectators – all of them standing on tip-toe as far as the heights there – the condemned man was laid under the Harrow by the Commandant himself. What is left today for a common soldier to do was then my task, the task of the presiding judge, and was an honour for me. And then the execution began! No discordant noise spoilt the working of the machine. Many did not care to watch it but lay with closed eyes in the sand; they all knew; now Justice is being done. In the silence one heard nothing but the condemned man's sighs, half muffled by the felt gag. Nowadays the machine can no longer wring from anyone a sigh louder than the felt gag can stifle; but in those days the writing needles let drop an acid fluid which we're not permitted to use today. Well, and then came the sixth hour! It was impossible to grant all the requests to be allowed to watch it from near by. The Commandant in his wisdom ordained that the children should have the preference; I, of course, because of my office had the privilege of always being at hand; often enough I would be squatting there with a small child in either arm. How we all absorbed the look of transfiguration on the face of the sufferer, how we bathed our cheeks in the radiance of that justice, achieved at last and fading so quickly! What times these were, my comrade!' The officer had obviously forgotten whom he was addressing; he had embraced the explorer and laid his head on his shoulder. The explorer was deeply embarrassed, impatiently he stared over the officer's head. The soldier had finished his cleaning job and was now pouring rice-pap from a pot into the basin. As soon as the condemned man, who seemed to have recovered himself entirely, noticed this action he began to reach for the rice with his tongue. The soldier kept pushing him away, since the rice-pap was certainly meant for a later hour, yet it was just as unfitting that the soldier himself should thrust his dirty hands into the basin and eat out of it, before the other's avid face.

The officer quickly pulled himself together. 'I didn't want to upset you,' he said, 'I know it is impossible to make those days credible now. Anyhow, the machine is still working and it is still effective in itself. It is effective in itself even though it stands alone in this valley. And the corpse still falls at the last into the grave with an incomprehensively gentle wafting motion, even although there are no hundreds of people swarming round like flies as formerly. In those days we had to put a strong fence round the grave; it has long since been torn down.'

The explorer wanted to withdraw his face from the officer and looked round at him random. The officer thought he was surveying the valley's desolation; so he seized him by the hands, turned him round to meet his eyes, and asked: 'Do you observe the shame of it?'

But the explorer said nothing. The officer left him alone for a little; with legs apart, hands on hips, he stood very still, gazing at the ground. Then he smiled encouragingly at the explorer and said: 'I was quite near you yesterday when the Commandant gave you the invitation. I heard him giving it. I know the Commandant. I divined at once what he was after. Although he is powerful enough to take measures against me, he doesn't dare to do it yet, but he certainly means to use your verdict against me, the verdict of an illustrious foreigner. He has calculated it carefully: this is your second day on the island, you did not know the old Commandant and his ways, you are conditioned by European ways of thought, perhaps you object on principle to capital punishment in general and to such mechanical instruments of death in particular, besides you will see that the execution has no support from the public, a shabby ceremony – carried out with a machine already somewhat old and worn – now, taking all that into consideration, would it not be likely (so thinks the Commandant) that you might disapprove of my methods? And if you disapprove, you wouldn't conceal the fact (I'm still speaking from the Commandant's point of view), for you are a man to feel confidence in your own well-tried conclusions? True, you have seen and learned to appreciate the peculiarities of many peoples, and so you would not be likely to take a strong line against our proceedings, as you might do in your own country. But the Commandant has no need of that. A casual, even an unguarded remark will be enough. It doesn't even need to represent what you really think, so long as it can be used speciously to serve his purpose. He will try to prompt you with sly questions, of that I am certain. And his ladies will sit around you and prick up their ears; you might be saying something like this: "In our country we have a different way of carrying out justice," or "In our country the prisoner has a chance to defend himself before he is sentenced," or "We haven't used torture since the Middle Ages." All these statements are as true as they seem natural to you, harmless remarks that pass no judgements on my methods. But how would the Commandant react to them? I can see him, our good Commandant, pushing his chair away immediately and rushing on to the balcony, I can see his ladies streaming out after him, I can hear his voice – the ladies call it a voice of thunder – well, and this is what he says: "A famous Western investigator, sent out to study criminal procedure in all the countries of the world, has just said that our old tradition of administering justice is inhumane. Such a verdict from such a personality makes it impossible for me to countenance these methods any longer. Therefore from this very day I ordain", and so on. You may want to interpose that you never said any such thing, that you never called my methods inhumane, on the contrary, your profound experience leads you to believe they are most humane and most in consonance with human dignity, and you admire the machine greatly – but it will be too late; you won't even get on to the balcony, crowded as it will be with ladies; you may try to draw attention to yourself; you may want to scream out; but a lady's hand will close your lips – and I and the old Commandant will be done for.'

The explorer had to suppress a smile; so easy, then, was the task he had felt to be so difficult. He said evasively: 'You overestimate my influence; the Commandant has read my letters of recommendation, he knows that I am no expert in criminal procedure. If I were to give an opinion, it would be as a private individual, an opinion no more influential than that of any ordinary person, and in any case much less influential than that of the Commandant, who, I am given to understand, has very extensive powers in this penal settlement. If his attitude to your procedure is as definitely hostile as you believe, then I fear the end of your tradition is at hand, even without any humble assistance from me.'

Had it dawned on the officer at last? No, he still did not understand. He shook his head emphatically, glanced briefly round at the condemned man and the soldier, who both flinched away from the rice, came close up to the explorer and without looking at his face but fixing his eye on some spot on his coat said in a lower voice than before: 'You don't know the Commandant; you feel yourself – forgive the expression – a kind of outsider so far as all of us are concerned; yet, believe me, your influence cannot be rated too highly. I was simply delighted when I heard that you were to attend the execution all by yourself. The Commandant arranged it to aim a blow at me, but I shall turn it to my advantage. Without being distracted by lying whispers and contemptuous glances – which could not have been avoided had a crowd of people attended the execution – you have heard my explanations, seen the machine, and are now in course of watching the execution. You have doubtless already formed your own judgement; if you still have some small uncertainties, the sight of the execution will resolve them. And now I make this request to you: Help me against the Commandant!' The explorer would not let him go on. 'How could I do that?' he cried, 'it's quite impossible. I can neither help nor hinder you.' 'Yes, you can,' said the officer. With certain apprehension the explorer saw that the officer had clenched his fists. 'Yes, you can,' repeated the officer, still more insistently. 'I have a plan that is bound to succeed. You believe your influence is insufficient. I know that it is sufficient. But even granted that you are right, is it not necessary, for the sake of preserving this tradition, to try even what might prove insufficient? Listen to my plan, then. The first thing necessary for you to carry it out is to be as reticent as possible regarding your verdict on these proceedings. Unless you are asked a direct question you must say nothing at all; but what you do say must be brief and general; let it be remarked that you would prefer not to discuss the matter, that you are out of patience with it, that if you were to let yourself go you would use strong language. I don't ask you to tell any lies; by no means; you should give only curt answers, such as: "Yes, I saw the execution," or "Yes, I had it explained to me." Just that, nothing more. There are grounds enough for any impatience you betray, although not such as will occur to the Commandant. Of course, he will mistake your meaning and interpret it to please himself. That's what my plan depends on. Tomorrow in the Commandant's office there is to be a large conference of all the high administrative officials, the Commandant presiding. Of course the Commandant is the kind of man to have turned these conferences into public spectacles. He has had a gallery built that is always packed with spectators. I am compelled to take part in the conferences, but they make me sick with nausea. Now, whatever happens, you will certainly be invited to this conference; if you behave today as I suggest the invitation will become an urgent request. But if for some mysterious reason you're not invited, you'll have to ask for an invitation: there's no doubt of your getting it then. So tomorrow you're sitting in the Commandant's box with the ladies. He keeps looking up to make sure you're there. After various trivial and ridiculous matters, brought in merely to impress the audience – mostly harbour works, nothing but harbour works! – our judicial procedure comes up for discussion too. If the Commandant doesn't introduce it, or not soon enough, I'll see that it's mentioned. I'll stand up and report that today's execution has taken place. Quite briefly, only a statement. Such a statement is not usual, but I shall make it. The Commandant thanks me, as always, with an amiable smile, and then he can't restrain himself, he seizes the excellent opportunity. "It has just been reported," he will say, or words to that effect, "that an execution has taken place. I should like merely to add that this execution was witnessed by the famous investigator who has, as you all know, honoured our colony so exceptionally by his visit to us. His presence at today's session of our conference also contributes to the importance of this occasion. Should we not now ask the famous investigator to give us his verdict on our traditional mode of execution and the procedure that leads up to it?" Of course there is loud applause, general agreement, I am more insistent than anyone. The Commandant bows to you and says: "Then in the name of the assembled company, I put the question to you." And now you advance to the front of the box. Lay your hands where everyone can see them, or the ladies will catch them and press your fingers. And then at last you can speak out. I don't know how I'm going to endure the tension of waiting for that moment. Don't put any restraint on yourself when you make your speech, publish the truth aloud, lean over the front of the box, shout, yes indeed, shout your verdict, your unshakable conviction, at the Commandant. Yet perhaps you wouldn't care to do that, it's not in keeping with your character, in your country perhaps people do these things differently, well, that's all right too, that will be quite as effective, don't even stand up, just say a few words, even in a whisper, so that only the officials beneath you will hear them, that will be quite enough, you don't even need to mention the lack of public support for the execution, the creaking wheel, the broken strap, the filthy stump of felt, no, I'll take all that upon me, and, believe me, if my indictment doesn't drive him out of the conference hall, it will force him to his knees to make the acknowledgement: "Old Commandant, I humble myself before you." That is my plan; will you help me to carry it out? But of course you are willing, what is more, you must.' And the officer seized the explorer by both arms and gazed, breathing heavily, into his face. He had shouted the last sentence so loudly that even the soldier and the condemned man were startled into attending; they had not understood a word but they stopped eating and looked over at the explorer, chewing their previous mouthfuls.

From the very beginning the explorer had no doubt about what answer he must give; in his lifetime he had experienced too much to have any uncertainty here; he was fundamentally honourable and unafraid. And yet now, facing the soldier and the condemned man, he did hesitate for as long as it took to draw one breath. At last, however, he said, as he had to: 'No.' The officer blinked several times but did not turn his eyes away. 'Would you like me to explain?' asked the explorer. The officer nodded, mutely. 'I do not approve of your procedure,' said the explorer then, 'even before you took me into your confidence – of course I shall never in any circumstances betray your confidence – I was already wondering whether it would be my duty to intervene and whether my intervention would have the slightest chance of success. I realized to whom I ought to turn: to the Commandant, of course. You have made that fact even clearer, but without having strengthened my resolution, on the contrary, your sincere conviction has touched me, even though it cannot influence my judgement.'

The officer remained mute, turned to the machine, caught hold of a brass rod, and then, leaning back a little, gazed at the Designer as if to assure himself that all was in order. The soldier and the condemned man seemed to have come to some understanding; the condemned man was making signs to the soldier, difficult though his movements were because of the tight straps; the soldier was bending down to him; the condemned man whispered something and the soldier nodded.

The explorer followed the officer and said: 'You don't know yet what I mean to do. I shall tell the Commandant what I think of the procedure, certainly, but not at a public conference, only in private; nor shall I stay here long enough to attend any conference; I am going away early tomorrow morning, or at least embarking on my ship.'

It did not look as if the officer had been listening. 'So you did not find the procedure convincing,' he said to himself and smiled, as an old man smiles at childish nonsense and yet pursues his own meditations behind the smile.

'Then the time has come,' he said at last and suddenly looked at the explorer with bright eyes that held some challenge, some appeal for cooperation. 'The time for what?' asked the explorer uneasily, but got no answer.

'You are free,' said the officer to the condemned man in the native tongue. The man did not believe it at first. 'Yes, you are set free,' said the officer. For the first time the condemned man's face woke to real animation. Was it true? Was it only a caprice of the officer's, that might change again? Had the foreign explorer begged him off? What was it? One could read these questions on his face. But not for long. Whatever it might be, he wanted to be really free if he might, and he began to struggle so far as the Harrow permitted him.

'You'll burst my straps,' cried the officer, 'lie still! We'll soon loosen them.' And signing the soldier to help him, he set about doing so. The condemned man laughed wordlessly to himself, now he turned his face left towards the officer, now right towards the soldier, nor did he forget the explorer.

'Draw him out,' ordered the officer. Because of the Harrow this had to be done with some care. The condemned man had already torn himself a little in the back through his impatience.

From now on, however, the officer paid hardly any attention to him. He went up to the explorer, pulled out the small leather brief-case again, turned over the papers in it, found the one he wanted and showed it to the explorer. 'Read it,' he said. 'I can't,' said the explorer, 'I told you before that I can't make out these scripts.' 'Try taking a close look at it,' said the officer and came quite near to the explorer so that they might read it together. But when even that proved useless, he outlined the script with his little finger, holding it high above the paper as if the surface dared not be sullied by touch, in order to help the explorer to follow the script in that way. The explorer did make an effort, meaning to please the officer in this respect at least, but he was quite unable to follow. Now the officer began to spell it, letter by letter, and then read out the words. '"BE JUST!" is what is written there,' he said, 'surely you can read it now.' The explorer bent so close to the paper that the officer feared he might touch it and drew it farther away; the explorer made no remark, yet it was clear that he still could not decipher it. '"Be just!" is what is written there,' said the officer once more. 'Maybe,' said the explorer, 'I am prepared to believe you.' 'Well, then,' said the officer, at least partly satisfied, and climbed up the ladder with the paper; very carefully he laid it inside the Designer and seemed to be changing the disposition of all the cog-wheels; it was a troublesome piece of work and must have involved wheels that were extremely small, for sometimes the officer's head vanished altogether from sight inside the Designer, so precisely did he have to regulate the machinery.

The explorer, down below, watched the labour uninterruptedly, his neck grew stiff, and his eyes smarted from the glare of sunshine over the sky. The soldier and the condemned man were now busy together. The man's shirt and trousers which were already lying in the grave, were fished out by the point of the soldier's bayonet. The shirt was abominably dirty and its owner washed it in the bucket of water. When he put on the shirt and trousers both he and the soldier could not help guffawing, for the garments were of course slit up behind. Perhaps the condemned man felt it incumbent on him to amuse the soldier, he turned round and round in his slashed garments before the soldier, who squatted on the ground beating his knees with mirth. All the same, they presently controlled their mirth out of respect for the gentlemen.

When the officer had at length finished his task aloft, he surveyed the machinery in all its details once more with a smile, but this time shut the lid of the Designer, which had stayed open till now, climbed down, looked into the grave and then at the condemned man, noting with satisfaction that the clothing had been taken out, then went over to wash his hands in the water-bucket, perceived too late that it was disgustingly dirty, was unhappy because he could not wash his hands, in the end thrust them into the sand – this alternative did not please him, but he had to put up with it – then stood upright and began to unbutton his uniform jacket. As he did this, the two ladies' handkerchiefs he had tucked at the back of his collar fell into his hands. 'Here are your handkerchiefs,' he said, and threw them to the condemned man. And to the explorer he said in explanation: 'A gift from the ladies.'

In spite of the obvious haste with which he was discarding first his uniform jacket and then all his clothing, he handled each garment with loving care, he even ran his fingers caressingly over the silver lace on the jacket and shook a tassel into place. This loving care was certainly out of keeping with the fact that as soon as he had a garment off he flung it at once with a kind of unwilling jerk into the grave. The last thing left to him was his small-sword with the sword-belt. He drew it out of the scabbard, broke it, then gathered all together, the bits of the sword, the scabbard and the belt, and flung them so violently down that they clattered into the grave.

Now he stood naked there. The explorer bit his lips and said nothing. He knew very well what was going to happen, but he had no right to obstruct the officer in anything. If the judicial procedure which the officer cherished were really so near its end – possibly as a result of the explorer's intervention, to which he felt himself pledged – then the officer was doing the right thing; in his place the explorer would not have acted otherwise.

The soldier and the condemned man did not understand at first what was happening, to begin with they were not even looking on. The condemned man was gleeful at having got the handkerchiefs back, but he was not allowed to enjoy them for long, since the soldier snatched them with a sudden, unexpected grab. Now the condemned man in turn was trying to twitch them from under the belt where the soldier had tucked them, but the soldier was on his guard. So they were wrestling, half in jest. Only when the officer stood quite naked was their attention caught. The condemned man especially seemed struck with the notion that a great change of fortune was impending. What had happened to him was now going to happen to the officer. Perhaps even to the very end. Apparently the foreign explorer had given the order for it. So this was revenge. Although he himself had not suffered to the end, he was to be revenged to the end. A broad, silent grin now appeared on his face and stayed there all the rest of the time.

The officer, however, had turned to the machine. It had been clear enough previously that he understood the machine well, but now it was almost staggering to see how he managed it and how it obeyed him. His hand had only to approach the Harrow for it to rise and sink several times till it was adjusted to the right position for receiving him; he touched only the edge of the Bed and already it was vibrating; the felt gag came to meet his mouth, one could see that the officer was really reluctant to take it, but he shrank from it only a moment, soon he submitted and received it. Everything was ready, only the straps hung down at the sides, yet they were obviously unnecessary, the officer did not need to be fastened down. Then the condemned man noticed the loose straps, in his opinion the execution was incomplete unless the straps were buckled, he gestured eagerly to the soldier and they ran together to strap the officer down. The latter had already stretched out one foot to push the lever that started the Designer; he saw the two men coming up, so he drew his foot back and let himself be buckled in. But now he could not reach the lever; neither the soldier nor the condemned man would be able to find it, and the explorer was determined not to lift a finger. It was not necessary; as soon as the straps were fastened the machine began to work; the Bed vibrated, the needles flickered above the skin, the Harrow rose and fell. The explorer had been staring at it quite a while before he remembered that a wheel in the Designer should have been creaking; but everything was quiet, not even the slightest hum could be heard.

Because it was working so silently the machine simply escaped one's attention. The explorer observed the soldier and the condemned man. The latter was the more animated of the two, everything in the machine interested him, now he was bending down and now stretching up on tip-toe, his forefinger was extended all the time pointing out details to the soldier. This annoyed the explorer. He was resolved to stay till the end, but he could not bear the sight of these two. 'Go back home,' he said. The soldier would have been willing enough, but the condemned man took the order as a punishment. With clasped hands he implored to be allowed to stay, and when the explorer shook his head and would not relent, he even went down on his knees. The explorer saw that it was no use merely giving orders, he was on the point of going over and driving them away. At that moment he heard a noise above him in the Designer. He looked up. Was that cog-wheel going to make trouble after all? But it was something quite different. Slowly the lid of the Designer rose up and then clicked wide open. The teeth of a cog-wheel showed themselves and rose higher, soon the whole wheel was visible, it was as if some enormous force were squeezing the Designer so that there was no longer room for the wheel, the wheel moved up till it came to the very edge of the Designer, fell down, rolled along the sand a little on its rim and then lay flat. But a second wheel was already rising after it, followed by many others, large and small and indistinguishably minute, the same thing happened to all of them, at every moment one imagined the Designer must now really be empty, but another complex of numerous wheels was already rising into sight, falling down, trundling along the sand and lying flat. This phenomenon made the condemned man completely forget the explorer's command, the cog-wheels fascinated him, he was always trying to catch one and at the same time urging the soldier to help, but always drew back his hand in alarm, for another wheel always came hopping along which, at least on its first advance, scared him off.

The explorer, on the other hand, felt greatly troubled; the machine was obviously going to pieces; its silent working was a delusion; he had a feeling that he must now stand by the officer since the officer was no longer able to look after himself. But while the tumbling cog-wheels absorbed his whole attention he had forgotten to keep an eye on the rest of the machine; now that the last cog-wheel had left the Designer, however, he bent over the Harrow and had a new and still more unpleasant surprise. The Harrow was not writing, it was only jabbing, and the Bed was not turning the body over but only bringing it up quivering against the needles. The explorer wanted to do something, if possible, to bring the whole machine to a standstill, for this was no exquisite torture such as the officer desired, this was plain murder. He stretched out his hands. But at that moment the Harrow rose with the body spitted on it and moved to the side, as it usually did only when the twelfth hour had come. Blood was flowing in a hundred streams, not mingled with water; the water-jets too had failed to function. And now the last action failed to fulfil itself, the body did not drop off the long needles, streaming with blood it went on hanging over the grave without falling into it. The Harrow tried to move back to its old position, but as if it had itself noticed that it had not yet got rid of its burden it stuck after all where it was, over the grave. 'Come and help!' cried the explorer to the other two, and himself seized the officer's feet. He wanted to push against the feet while the others seized the head from the opposite side and so the officer might be slowly eased off the needles. But the other two could not make up their minds to come; the condemned man actually turned away; the explorer had to go over to them and force them into position at the officer's head. And here, almost against his will, he had to look at the face of the corpse. It was as it had been in life; no sign was visible of the promised redemption; what the others had found in the machine the officer had not found; the lips were firmly pressed together, the eyes were open, with the same expression as in life, their look was calm and convinced, through the forehead went the point of the great iron spike.

*

As the explorer, with the soldier and the condemned man behind him, reached the first houses of the settlement, the soldier pointed to one of them and said: 'There is the tea-house.'

In the ground floor of the house was a deep, low, cavernous space, its walls and ceiling blackened with smoke. It was open to the road all along its length. Although this tea-house was very little different from the other houses of the settlement, which were all very dilapidated, even up to the Commandant's palatial headquarters, it made on the explorer the impression of a historic tradition of some kind, and he felt the power of past days. He went near to it, followed by his companions, right up between the empty tables which stood in the road before it, and breathed the cool heavy air that came from the interior. 'The old man's buried here,' said the soldier, 'the priest wouldn't let him lie in the churchyard. Nobody knew where to bury him for a while, but in the end they buried him here. The officer never told you about that, for sure, because of course that's what he was most ashamed of. He even tried several times to dig the old man up by night, but he was always chased away.'

'Where is the grave?' asked the explorer, who found it impossible to believe the soldier. At once both of them, the soldier and the condemned man, ran before him pointing with outstretched hands in the direction where the grave should be. They led the explorer right up to the back wall, where guests were sitting at a few tables. These were apparently dock labourers, strong men with short, glistening, full black beards. None had a jacket, their shirts were torn, they were poor, humble creatures. As the explorer drew near some of them got up, pressed close to the wall, and stared at him. 'It's a stranger,' ran the whisper around him, 'he wants to see the grave.' They pushed one of the tables aside, and under it there was really a grave-stone. It was a simple stone, low enough to be covered by a table. There was an inscription on it in very small letters, the explorer had to kneel down to read it. This was what it said: 'Here rests the old Commandant. His adherents, who now must be nameless, have dug this grave and set up this stone. There is a prophecy that after a certain number of years the Commandant will rise again and lead his adherents from this house to recover the colony. Have faith and wait!' When the explorer had read this and risen to his feet he saw all the bystanders around him smiling, as if they too had read the inscription, had found it ridiculous and were expecting him to agree with them. The explorer ignored this, distributed a few coins among them, waited till the table was pushed over the grave again, quitted the tea-house and made for the harbour.

The soldier and the condemned man had found some acquaintances in the tea-house, who detained them. But they must have soon shaken them off, for the explorer was only half-way down the long flight of steps leading to the boats when they came rushing after him. Probably they wanted to force him at the last minute to take them with him. While he was bargaining below with a ferryman to row him to the steamer, the two of them came headlong down the steps, in silence, for they did not dare to shout. But by the time they reached the foot of the steps the explorer was already in the boat, and the ferryman was just casting off from the shore. They could have jumped into the boat, but the explorer lifted a heavy knotted rope from the floor-boards, threatened them with it, and so kept them from attempting the leap.

The Giant Mole

THOSE, and I am one of them, who find even a small ordinary sized mole disgusting, would probably have died of disgust if they had seen the great mole that a few years back was observed in the neighbourhood of one of our villages, which achieved a certain transitory celebrity on account of the incident. Today it has long since sunk back into oblivion again, and in that only shares the obscurity of the whole incident, which has remained quite inexplicable, but which people, it must be confessed, have also taken no great pains to explain; and so, as the result of an incomprehensible apathy in those very circles which should have concerned themselves with it, and who in fact have shown enthusiastic interest in far more trifling matters, the affair has been forgotten without ever being adequately investigated. In any case the fact that the village could not be reached by the railroad was no excuse. Many people came from great distances out of pure curiosity, there were even foreigners among them; it was only those who should have shown something more than curiosity that refrained from coming. In fact, if a few quite simple people, people whose daily work gave them hardly a moment of leisure – if these people had not quite disinterestedly taken up the affair, the rumour of this natural phenomenon would probably have never spread beyond the locality. Indeed, rumour itself, which usually cannot be held within bounds, was actually sluggish in this case; if it had not literally been given a shove it would not have spread. But even that was no valid reason for refusing to inquire into the affair; on the contrary this second phenomenon should have been investigated as well. Instead the old village teacher was left to write the sole account of the incident in black and white, and though he was an excellent man in his own profession his abilities and his equipment alike rendered it impossible for him to produce an exhaustive description that could be used as a foundation by others, far less, therefore, an actual explanation of the occurrence. His little pamphlet was printed, and a good few copies were sold to visitors to the village about that time; it also received some public recognition, but the teacher was wise enough to perceive that his fragmentary labours, in which no one supported him, were at bottom without value. If in spite of that he did not relax in them, and made the question his life work, though it naturally became more hopeless from year to year, that only shows on the one hand how powerful an effect the appearance of the great mole was capable of producing, and on the other how much laborious effort and fidelity to his convictions may be found in an old and obscure village teacher. But that he suffered deeply from the cold attitude of the recognized authorities is proved by a brief brochure with which he followed up his pamphlet several years later, by which time hardly any one could remember what it was all about. In this brochure he complained of the lack of understanding that he had encountered in people where it was least to be expected; complaints which carried conviction less by the skill with which they were expressed than by their honesty. Of such people he said very appositely: 'It is not I, but they, who talk like old village teachers.' And among other things he adduced the pronouncement of a scholar to whom he had gone expressly about his affair. The name of the scholar was not mentioned, but from various circumstances we could guess who it was. After the teacher had managed with great difficulty to secure admittance, he perceived at once from the very way in which he was greeted that the savant had already acquired a rooted prejudice against the matter. The absence with which he listened to the long report which the teacher, pamphlet in hand, delivered to him, can be gauged from a remark that he let fall after a pause for ostensible reflection: 'The soil in your neighbourhood is particularly black and rich. Consequently it provides the moles with particularly rich nourishment, and so they grow to an unusual size.'

'But not to such a size as that!' exclaimed the teacher, and he measured off two yards on the wall, somewhat exaggerating the length of the mole in his exasperation. 'Oh, and why not?' replied the scholar, who obviously looked upon the whole affair as a great joke. With this verdict the teacher had to return to his home. He tells how his wife and six children were waiting for him by the roadside in the snow, and how he had to admit to them the final collapse of his hopes.

When I read of the scholar's attitude towards the old man I was not yet acquainted with the teacher's pamphlet. But I at once resolved myself to collect and correlate all the information I could discover regarding the case. If I could not employ physical force against the scholar, I could at least write a defence of the teacher, or more exactly, of the good intentions of an honest but uninfluential man. I admit that I rued this decision later, for I soon saw that its execution was bound to involve me in a very strange predicament. On the one hand my own influence was far from sufficient to effect a change in learned or even public opinion in the teacher's favour, while on the other the teacher was bound to notice that I was less concerned with his main object, which was to prove that the great mole had actually been seen, than to defend his honesty, which must naturally be self-evident to him and in need of no defence. Accordingly, what was bound to happen was this: I would be misunderstood by the teacher, though I wanted to collaborate with him, and instead of helping him I myself would probably require support, which was unlikely to be given. Besides, my decision would impose a great burden of work upon me. If I wanted to convince people I could not invoke the teacher, since he himself had not been able to convince them. To read his pamphlet could only have led me astray, and so I refrained from reading it until I should have finished my own labours. More, I did not even get in touch with the teacher. True, he heard of my inquiries through intermediaries, but he did not know whether I was working for him or against him. In fact he probably assumed the latter, though he denied it later on; for I have proof of the fact that he put various obstacles in my way. It was quite easy for him to do that, for of course I was compelled to undertake anew all the inquiries he had already made, and so he could always steal a march on me. But that was the only objection that could be justly made to my method, an unavoidable reproach, moreover, which the caution and self-abnegation with which I drew my conclusions palliated still more. But for the rest my pamphlet was quite influenced by the teacher, perhaps on this point, indeed, I showed all too great a scrupulosity; from my words one might have thought nobody whatever had inquired into the case before, and I was the first to interrogate those who had seen or heard of the mole, the first to correlate the evidence, the first to draw conclusions. When later I read the teacher's pamphlet – it had a very circumstantial title: 'A mole, larger in size than any ever seen before' – I found that we actually did not agree on certain important points, though we both believed we had proved our main point, namely, the existence of the mole. These differences prevented the establishment of the friendly relations with the teacher that I had been looking forward to in spite of everything. On his side there developed a feeling almost of hostility. True, he was always modest and humble in his bearing towards me, but that only made his real feelings the more obvious. In other words, he was of the opinion that I had merely damaged his credit, and that my belief that I had been or could be of assistance to him was simplicity at best, but more likely presumption or artifice. He was particularly fond of saying that all his previous enemies had shown their hostility either not at all, or in private, or at most by word of mouth, while I had considered it necessary to have my censures straightway published. Moreover, the few opponents of his who had really occupied themselves with the subject, if but superficially, had at least listened to his, the teacher's views, before they had given expression to their own; while I, on the strength of unsystematically assembled and in part misunderstood evidence, had published conclusions which, even if they were correct as regarded the main point, must evoke incredulity, and among the public no less than the educated. But the faintest hint that the existence of the mole was unworthy of credence was the worst thing that could happen in this case.

To these reproaches, veiled as they were, I could easily have found an answer – for instance, that his own pamphlet achieved the very summit of the incredible – it was less easy, however, to make headway against his continual suspicion, and that was the reason why I was very reserved in my dealings with him. For in his heart he was convinced that I wanted to rob him of the fame of being the first man publicly to vindicate the mole. Now of course he really enjoyed no fame whatever, but only an absurd notoriety that was shrinking more and more, and for which I had certainly no desire to compete. Besides, in the foreword to my pamphlet I had expressly declared that the teacher must stand for all time as the discoverer of the mole – and he was not even that – and that only my sympathy with his unfortunate fate had spurred me on to write. 'It is the aim of this pamphlet' – so I ended up all too melodramatically, but it corresponded with my feelings at that time – 'to help in giving the teacher's book the wide publicity it deserves. If I succeed in that, then may my name, which I regard as only transiently and indirectly associated with this question, be blotted from it at once.' Thus I disclaimed expressly any major participation in the affair; it was almost as if I had foreseen in some manner the teacher's unbelievable reproaches. Nevertheless he found in that very passage a handle against me, and I do not deny that there was a faint show of justice in what he said or rather hinted; indeed I was often struck by the fact that he showed almost a keener penetration where I was concerned than he had done in his pamphlet. For he maintained that my foreword was double-faced. If I was really concerned solely to give publicity to his pamphlet, why had I not occupied myself exclusively with him and his pamphlet, why had I not pointed out its virtues, its irrefutability, why had I not confined myself to insisting on the significance of the discovery and making that clear, why had I instead tackled the discovery itself, while completely ignoring the pamphlet? Had not the discovery been made already? Was there still anything left to be done in that direction? But if I really thought that it was necessary for me to make the discovery all over again, why had I emphasized the original discovery so solemnly in my foreword? One might put that down to false modesty, but it was something worse. I was trying to belittle the discovery, I was drawing attention to it merely for the purpose of depreciating it, while he on the other hand had inquired into and finally established it. Perhaps the affair had sunk somewhat into oblivion; now I had made a noise about it again, but at the same time I had made the teacher's position more difficult than ever. What did he care whether his honesty was vindicated or not? All that he was concerned with was the thing itself, and with that alone. But I was only of disservice to it, for I did not understand it, I did not prize it at its true value, I had not real feeling for it. It was infinitely above my intellectual capacity. He sat before me and looked at me, his old wrinkled face quite composed, and yet this was what he was thinking. Yet it was not true that he was only concerned with the thing itself: actually he was very greedy for fame, and wanted to make money out of the business too, which, however, considering his large family, was very understandable. Nevertheless my interest in the affair seemed so trivial compared with his own, that he felt he could claim to be completely disinterested without deviating very seriously from the truth. And indeed my inner doubts refused to be quite calmed by my telling myself that the man's reproaches were really due to the fact that he clung to his mole, so to speak, with both hands, and was bound to look upon anyone who laid even a finger on it as a traitor.

For that was not true; his attitude was not to be explained by greed, or at any rate by greed alone, but rather by the touchiness which his great labours and their complete unsuccess had bred in him. Yet even his touchiness did not explain everything. Perhaps my interest in the affair was really too trivial. The teacher was used to lack of interest in strangers. He regarded it as a universal evil, but no longer suffered from its individual manifestations. Now a man had appeared who, strangely enough, took up the affair and even he did not understand it. Attacked from this side I can make no defence. I am no zoologist; yet perhaps I would have thrown myself into the case with my whole heart if I had discovered it; but I had not discovered it. Such a gigantic mole is certainly a prodigy, yet one cannot expect the continuous and undivided attention of the whole world to be accorded it, particularly if its existence is not completely and irrefutably established, and in any case it cannot be produced. And I admit too that even if I had been the discoverer I would probably never have come forward so gladly and voluntarily in defence of the mole as I had in that of the teacher.

Now the misunderstanding between me and the teacher would probably have quickly cleared up if my pamphlet had achieved success. But success was not forthcoming. Perhaps the book was not well-enough written, not persuasive enough; I am a business man, it may be that the composition of such a pamphlet was still further beyond my limited powers than those of the teacher, though in the kind of knowledge required I was greatly superior to him. Besides, my unsuccess may be explicable in other ways; the time at which the pamphlet appeared may have been inauspicious. The discovery of the mole, which had failed to penetrate to a wide public at the time it took place, was not so long past on the one hand as to be completely forgotten, and thus capable of being brought alive again by my pamphlet, while on the other hand enough time had elapsed quite to exhaust the trivial interest that had originally existed.

Those who took my pamphlet at all seriously told themselves, in that bored tone which from the first had characterized the debate, that now the old useless labours on this wearisome question were to begin all over again; and some even confused my pamphlet with the teacher's. In a leading agricultural journal appeared the following comment, fortunately at the very end, and in small print: 'The pamphlet on the giant mole has once more been sent to us. Years ago we remember having had a hearty laugh over it. Since then it has not become more intelligible, nor we more hard of understanding. But we simply refuse to laugh at it a second time. Instead, we would ask our teaching associations whether more useful work cannot be found for our village teachers than hunting out giant moles.' An unpardonable confusion of identity. They had read neither the first nor the second pamphlet, and the two perfunctorily scanned expressions, 'giant mole' and 'village teacher', were sufficient for these gentlemen, as representatives of publicly esteemed interests, to pronounce on the subject. Against this attack measures might have been attempted and with success, but the lack of understanding between the teacher and myself kept me from venturing upon them. I tried instead to keep the review from his knowledge as long as I could. But he very soon discovered it, as I recognized from a sentence in one of his letters, in which he announced his intention of visiting me for the Christmas holidays. He wrote: 'The world is full of malice, and people smooth the path for it,' by which he wished to convey that I was one of the malicious, but, not content with my own innate malice, wished also to make the world's path smooth for it: in other words, was acting in such a way as to arouse the general malice and help it to victory. Well, I summoned the resolution I required, and was able to await him calmly, and calmly greet him when he arrived, this time a shade less polite in his bearing than usual; he carefully drew out the journal from the breast-pocket of his old-fashioned padded overcoat, and opening it handed it to me. 'I've seen it,' I replied, handing

the journal back unread. 'You've seen it,' he said with a sigh;
he had the old teacher's habit of repeating unwelcome answers.
'Of course I won't take this lying down!' he went on, tapping
the journal excitedly with his finger and glancing up sharply at
me, as if I were of a different mind; he certainly had some idea
of what I was about to say, for I think I have noticed, not so
much from his words as from other indications, that he often
has a genuine intuition of my wishes, though he never yields to
them or lets himself be diverted from his aims. What I said to
him I can set down almost word for word, for I took a note of
it shortly after our interview. 'Do what you like,' I said, 'our
ways part from this moment. I fancy that that is neither unexpected nor unwelcome news to you. The review in this journal
is not the real reason for my decision; it has merely finally confirmed it. The real reason is this: originally I thought my intervention might be of some use to you, while now I cannot but
recognize that I have damaged you in every direction. Why it
has turned out so I cannot say; the cause of success and unsuccess are always ambiguous; but don't look for the sole explanation in my shortcomings. Consider; you too had the best
intentions, and yet, if one regards the matter objectively, you
failed. I don't intend it as a joke, for it would be a joke against
myself, when I say that your connexion with me must unfortunately be counted among your failures. It is neither cowardice
nor treachery, if I withdraw from the affair now. Actually it
involves a certain degree of self-renunciation; my pamphlet itself proves how much I respect you personally, in a certain sense
you have become my teacher, and I have almost grown fond of
the mole itself. Nevertheless I have decided to step aside; you
are the discoverer, and all that I can do is to prevent you from
gaining possible fame, while I attract failure and pass it on to
you. At least that is your own opinion. Enough of that. The
sole expiation that I can make is to beg your forgiveness and,
should you require it, to publish openly, that is, in this journal,
the admission I have just made to yourself.'

These were my words; they were not entirely sincere, but the sincerity in them was obvious enough. My explanation had the effect upon him that I had roughly anticipated. Most old people have something deceitful, something perfidious, in their dealing with people younger than themselves; you live at peace with them, imagine you are on the best of terms with them, know their ruling prejudices, receive continual assurances of amity, take the whole thing for granted; and when something decisive happens and those peaceful relations, so long nourished, should come into effective operation, suddenly these old people rise before you like strangers, show that they have deeper and stronger convictions, and now for the first time literally unfurl their banner, and with terror you read upon it the new decree. The reason for this terror lies chiefly in the fact that what the old say now is really far more just and sensible than what they said before; it is as if even the self-evident had degrees of validity, and their words now were more self-evident than ever. But the final deceit that lies in their words consists in this, that at bottom they have always said what they are saying now. I must have probed deeply into the teacher, seeing that his next words did not entirely take me by surprise. 'Child,' he said, laying his hand on mine and patting it gently, 'how did you ever take it into your head to go into this affair? – The very first I heard of it I talked it over with my wife.' He pushed his chair back from the table, got up, spread out his arms, and stared at the floor, as if his tiny little wife were standing there and he were speaking to her. 'We've struggled on alone,' he said to her, 'for many years; now, it seems, a noble protector has risen for us in the city, a fine business man, Mr So-and-so. We should congratulate ourselves, shouldn't we? A business man in the city isn't to be sniffed at; when an ignorant peasant believes us and says so it doesn't help us, for what a peasant may say or do is of no account; whether he says the old village teacher is right, or spits to show his contempt, the net result is the same. And if instead of one peasant ten thousand should stand up for us, the result, if possible, would only be still worse. A business man in the city, on the other hand, is quite a different pair of shoes; a man like that has connexions, things he says in passing, as it were, are taken up and repeated, new patrons interest themselves in the question, one of them, it may be, remarks: "You can learn even from old village teachers," and next day whole crowds of people are saying it to one another, people you would never imagine saying such things, to look at them. Next, money is found to finance the business, one gentleman goes round collecting for it and the others shower subscriptions on him; they decide that the village teacher must be dragged from his obscurity; they arrive, they don't bother about his external appearance, but take him to their bosoms, and since his wife and children depend on him, they accept them too. Have you ever watched city people? They chatter without stopping. When there's a whole lot of them together you can hear their chatter running from right to left and back again, and up and down, this way and that. And so, chattering away, they push us into the coach, so that we've hardly time to bow to everybody. The gentleman on the driver's seat puts his glasses straight, flourishes his whip, and off we go. They all wave a parting greeting to the village, as if we were still there and not sitting among them. The more important city people drive out in carriages to meet us. As we approach they get up from their seats and crane their necks. The gentleman who collected the money arranges everything methodically and in order. When we drive into the city we are a long procession of carriages. We think the public welcome is over; but it really only begins when we reach our hotel. A great crowd gathers as soon as our arrival is announced. What interests one interests all the rest immediately. They take their views from one another and promptly make those views their own. All the people who haven't managed to drive out and meet us in carriages, are waiting in front of the hotel; others could have driven out, but they were too self-conscious. They're waiting too. It's extraordinary, the way that the gentleman who collected the money keeps his eye on everything and directs everything.'

I had listened coolly to him, indeed I had grown cooler and cooler while he went on. On the table I had piled up all the copies of my pamphlet in my possession. Only a few were missing, for during the past week I had sent out a circular demanding the return of all the copies distributed, and had received most of them back. True, from several quarters I had got very polite notes saying that So-and-so could not remember having received such a pamphlet, and that, if it had actually arrived, he was sorry to confess that he must have lost it. Even that was gratifying; in my heart I desired nothing better. Only one reader begged me to let him keep the pamphlet as a curiosity, pledging himself, in accordance with the spirit of my circular, to show it to no one for twenty years. The village teacher had not yet seen my circular. I was glad that his words made it so easy for me to show it him. I could do that without anxiety in any case, however, as I had drawn it up very circumspectly, keeping his interests in mind the whole time. The crucial passage in the circular ran as follows: 'I do not ask for the return of the pamphlet because I retract in any way the opinions defended there or wish them to be regarded as erroneous or even undemonstrable on any point. My request has purely personal and moreover very urgent grounds; but no conclusion whatever must be drawn from it as regards my attitude to the whole matter. I beg to draw your particular attention to this, and would be glad also if you would make the fact better known.'

For the time being I kept my hand over the circular and said: 'You reproach me in your heart because things have not turned out as you hoped. Why do that? Don't let us embitter our last moments together. And do try to see that, though you've made a discovery, it isn't necessarily greater than every other discovery, and consequently the injustice you suffer under any greater than other injustices. I don't know the ways of learned societies, but I can't believe that in the most favourable circumstances you would have been given a reception even remotely resembling the one you seem to have described to your wife. While I myself still hoped that something might come of my pamphlet, the most I expected was that perhaps the attention of a professor might be drawn to our case, that he might commission some young student to inquire into it, that this student might visit you and check in his own fashion your and my inquiries once more on the spot, and that finally, if the results seemed to him worth consideration – we must not forget that all young students are full of scepticism – he might bring out a pamphlet of his own in which your discoveries would be put on a scientific basis. All the same, even if that hope had been realized nothing very much would still have been achieved. The student's pamphlet, supporting such queer opinions, would probably be held up to ridicule. If you take this agricultural journal as a sample, you can see how easily that may happen; and scientific periodicals are still more unscrupulous in such matters. And that's quite understandable; professors bear a great responsibility towards themselves, towards science, towards posterity; they can't take every new discovery to their bosoms straight away. We others have the advantage of them there. But I'll leave that out of account and assume that the student's pamphlet has found acceptance. What would happen next? You would probably receive honourable mention, the fact that you are a teacher possibly would go in your favour; people would say: "Our village teachers have sharp eyes"; and this journal, if journals have a memory or a conscience, would be forced to make you a public apology; also some well-intentioned professor would be found to secure a scholarship for you; it's possible they might even get you to come to the city, find a post for you in some school, and so give you a chance of using the scientific resources of a city so as to improve yourself. But if I am to be quite frank, I think they would content themselves with merely trying to do all this.

They would summon you and you would appear, but only as an ordinary petitioner like hundreds of others, and not in solemn state; they would talk to you and praise your honest efforts, but they would see at the same time that you were an old man, that it was hopeless for any one to begin to study science at such an age, and moreover that you had hit upon your discovery more by chance than by design, and had besides no ambition to extend your labours beyond this one case. For these reasons they would probably send you back to your village again. Your discovery, of course, would be carried further, for it is not so trifling that, once having achieved recognition, it could be forgotten again. But you would not hear much more about it, and what you heard you would scarcely understand. Every new discovery is assumed at once into the sum-total of knowledge, and with that ceases in a sense to be a discovery; it dissolves into the whole and disappears, and one must have a trained scientific eye even to recognize it after that. For it is related to fundamental axioms of whose existence we don't even know, and in the debates of science it is raised on these axioms into the very clouds. How can we expect to understand such things? Often as we listen to some learned discussion we may be under the impression that it is about your discovery, when it is about something quite different, and the next time, when we think it is about something else, and not about your discovery at all, it may turn out to be about that and that alone.

'Don't you see that? You would remain in your village, you would be able with the extra money to feed and clothe your family a little better; but your discovery would be taken out of your hands, and without your being able with any show of justice to object; for only in the city could it be given its final seal. And people wouldn't be altogether ungrateful to you, they might build a little museum on the spot where the discovery was made, it would become one of the sights of the village, you would be given the keys to keep, and, so that you shouldn't lack some outward token of honour, they could give you a little medal to wear on the breast of your coat, like those worn by attendants in scientific institutions. All this might have been possible; but was it what you wanted?'

Without stopping to consider his answer he turned on me and said: 'And so that's what you wanted to achieve for me?'

'Probably,' I said, 'I didn't consider what I was doing carefully enough at the time to be able to answer that clearly now. I wanted to help you, but that was a failure, and the worst failure I have ever had. That's why I want to withdraw now and undo what I've done as far as I'm able.'

'Well and good,' said the teacher, taking out his pipe and beginning to fill it with the tobacco that he carried loose in all his pockets. 'You took up this thankless business of your own free will, and now of your own free will you withdraw. So that's all right.'

'I'm not an obstinate man,' I said. 'Do you find anything to object to in my proposal?'

'No, absolutely nothing,' said the teacher, and his pipe was already going. I could not bear the stink of his tobacco, and so I rose and began to walk up and down the room. From previous encounters I was used to the teacher's extreme taciturnity, and to the fact that in spite of it he never seemed to have any desire to stir from my room once he was in it. That had often disturbed me before. He wants something more, I always thought at such times, and I would offer him money, which indeed he invariably accepted. Yet he never went away before it suited his convenience. Generally his pipe was smoked out by that time, then he would ceremoniously and respectfully push his chair in to the table, make a detour round it, seize his ash plant standing in the corner, press my hand warmly, and go. But today his silent presence as he sat there was an actual torture to me. When one has bidden a last farewell to someone, as I had done, a farewell accepted in good faith, surely the mutual formalities that remain should be got over as quickly as possible, and one should not burden one's host purposelessly with one's silent presence. As I contemplated the stubborn little old fellow from behind, while he sat at the table, it seemed an impossible idea ever to show him the door.

MORE ABOUT PENGUINS

Penguinews, which appears every month, contains details of all the new books issued by Penguins as they are published. From time to time it is supplemented by *Penguins in Print*, which is a complete list of all available books published by Penguins. (There are well over three thousand of these.)

A specimen copy of *Penguinews* will be sent to you free on request, and you can become a subscriber for the price of the postage. For a year's issues (including the complete lists) please send 30p if you live in the United Kingdom, or 60p if you live elsewhere. Just write to Dept EP, Penguin Books Ltd, Harmondsworth, Middlesex, enclosing a cheque or postal order, and your name will be added to the mailing list.

Some other books published by Penguins are described on the following pages.

Note: *Penguinews* and *Penguins in Print* are not available in the U.S.A. or Canada

THOMAS MANN

Confessions of Felix Krull

'Here is that unheard of, that supposedly impossible thing, a good German comic novel – a marvellously good one' – Edwin Muir in the *Listener*

Buddenbrooks

'Has extraordinary value as a document over and above its importance as literature. The friendly dispassionateness of the book, the amplitude, the final perfection of clearness, make it as satisfying as a Dürer drawing' – *Observer*

Death in Venice

Apart from the title story, this volume contains two others of the author's widely known short works: *Tristan* and *Tonio Kröger*. *Death in Venice* tells of the tragic homosexual passion of a writer for a young Polish boy.

The Magic Mountain

A cosmopolitan collection of people are confined in a sanatorium high in the Swiss Alps. In spite of their isolation, love, war, and emotions all affect and influence their conversation, and they stand as a microcosm of the sick European society which lies below them.

The Holy Sinner

An epic of arch-sinfulness – witting and unwitting – based on the life of Grigorss, natural child of the Duke of Flanders by his sister, who after various adventures inadvertently married his own mother, but after many years of solitary penance was proclaimed Pope in Rome.

Doctor Faustus

One of the most convincing accounts of genius ever written. Thomas Mann charts Leverkühn's extraordinary career from his precocious childhood to his tragic death – when Leverkühn reveals the horrifying price he had to pay for his achievement.

Lotte in Weimar

The little provincial court of Weimar – a post-Waterloo Athens, agog with gossip and cerebral activity – is brilliantly recreated. But *Lotte in Weimar* is memorable, above all, for Mann's masterly portrayal of a creative genius, polymath and politician, and his influence on his contemporaries.

Also available
Little Herr Friedemann and Other Stories
Mario and the Magician and Other Stories

Not for sale in the U.S.A. or Canada

ROADS TO FREEDOM

JEAN-PAUL SARTRE'S TRILOGY IN PENGUINS

The Age of Reason

This novel covers two days in the life of Mathieu Delarue, a teacher of philosophy, and in the lives of his acquaintances and friends. Individual tragedies and happiness are etched against the Paris summer of 1938, with its night clubs, galleries, students, and café society.

But behind it all there is a threat, only half realized at the time, of the coming catastrophe of the Second World War.

'Constantly delights with its brilliance' – *Spectator*

'A dynamic, deeply disturbing novel' – Elizabeth Bowen

The Reprieve

The Reprieve includes many of the characters of *The Age of Reason*. It surveys that heat-wave week in September 1938, when Europe waited tensely for the result of the Munich conference. Sartre's technique of almost simultaneous description of several scenes enables him to suggest the mood of all Europe as it tried hard to blinker itself against the threat of war.

'His method is consummately able. It is only a writer with an exquisite sense of rhythm who can mix episode with episode as M. Sartre does here' – *Observer*

Iron in the Soul

In *Iron in the Soul* the same characters at last face reality, in the shape of defeat and occupation. Around a graphic narrative of the fall of France, Sartre weaves a tapestry of thoughts, feelings, and incidents which portrays – as few books about war have done – the meaning of defeat. As in the earlier books, the schoolmaster Mathieu is the most articulate character: able to reflect on the nature of freedom even as he fires his last rounds against the oncoming enemy.

Also available

WORDS

NAUSEA

Not for sale in the U.S.A.

HERMANN HESSE

Hermann Hesse (1877–1962), novelist and poet, won many literary awards including the Nobel prize (1946). He was interested in both psychology and Indian mysticism and his novels explore different attempts to find a 'total reality' in life.

Steppenwolf

This Faust-like, poetical and magical story of the humanization of a middle-aged misanthrope was described in the *New York Times* as 'a savage indictment of bourgeois society'. But, as the author notes in this edition, *Steppenwolf* is a book which has been violently mis-understood. This self-portrait of a man who felt himself to be half-human and half-wolf can also be seen as a plea for rigorous self-examination and an indictment of intellectual hypocrisy.

Narziss and Goldmund

Narziss is a teacher at Mariabronn, a monastery in medieval Germany. Brilliant and severe, he feels that Goldmund, his favourite pupil, will never be a scholar or a monk.

So Narziss helps Goldmund realize that they must each fulfil them-selves in different ways: Narziss retiring from the world into a patterned order of prayer and philosophy while Goldmund quits the cloisters to plunge into a sea of blood and lust; cutting a picaresque swathe through plague, storm and murder; always chasing a fugitive vision of artistic perfection, its form 'the mother of all things'.

In a sense, both Narziss and Goldmund – the ascetic and the Diony-sian – are what Hesse himself might have been. This element of con-jectural autobiography gives to this masterpiece a ripe wisdom, an insight into universal dilemmas and man's role on earth, unique in the fiction of our time.

Not for sale in the U.S.A.

FRANZ KAFKA

The work of this strange and enigmatic Czech author, who died of consumption in 1924, has earned him a unique reputation in modern European literature and has provoked many endeavours to interpret his view of life.

The Trial

Kafka elucidates some fundamental dilemmas of human life in this account of the perplexing experience of a man arrested on a charge which is never specified. The story reads like the transcript of a protracted, implacable dream in which reality is entangled with imagination.

The Castle

Here the world of Kafka is further illumined; the individual struggles against ubiquitous, elusive and anonymous powers determining and yet simultaneously opposing his every step.

America

America is the lightest and most realistic of Kafka's novels. Yet beneath the surface comedy of young Karl Rossman's discovery of America, the author hints at much more than he seems to be saying.

The Diaries of Franz Kafka

Kafka's diaries, edited by Max Brod, his lifelong friend, cover the period from 1910 to 1923 and reveal to us the extraordinary inner world in which he lived, his fear, isolation, frustration, feelings of guilt and his sense of being an outcast.

Not for sale in the U.S.A. or Canada